Playing Soccer
the Professional Way

Playing Soccer the Professional Way

**by Gordon Bradley
and Clive Toye**

of the New York Cosmos

Photographs by Paul Bereswill

Drawings by Mary Puschak

Harper & Row, Publishers

New York   Evanston   San Francisco   London

FIRST EDITION

Library of Congress Cataloging in Publication Data

Bradley, Gordon.
    Playing soccer the professional way.
    1. Soccer.   I. Toye, Clive, joint author.
II. Title
GV943.B68   796.33′4   73–4131
ISBN 0–06–010442–2

Contents

1 Soccer—The International Game 1

2 The Equipment and Players 15

3 The Basic Technique of Soccer:
Kicking 29

4 Ball Control and Other Soccer Basics 51

5 Techniques of Goalkeeping 87

6 Team Play and Systems of Play 105

7 A Team on Attack 121

8 A Team on Defense 153

9 Physical Fitness and Soccer Practice 169

10 Soccer and the American Player 187

Glossary 197

Appendix FIFA Official Rules of Soccer 201

Index 213

1

Soccer— The International Game

SOCCER never sleeps. It is the world's most popular participant and spectator sport, played in every time zone by men and boys (and, lest we're accused of male chauvinism, let's add "by women and girls") of every shape, size, and hue on earth.

Wherever you might be, right now, and whatever time it is as you read these words, someone, somewhere is playing soccer—maybe it's a bunch of boys on a bare lot in Iceland or Spain or Russia or Japan; or maybe in London or Milan, Buenos Aires or Moscow, Mexico City or Pyongyang, or in scores of cities in between, a crowd of one hundred thousand or more is watching some of the world's most highly skilled, and among the highest paid, athletes.

If it happens to be the right time in Rio de Janeiro, there could be up to a quarter of a million Cariocas thronging Maracana Stadium. It was there, in 1950, that over two hundred thousand people paid to see the World Cup Final between Brazil and Uruguay—the largest attendance in all of sports. Yet even that was dwarfed by the total viewing audience—in person and by television throughout the world—of the 1970 World Cup Final between Brazil and Italy in Mexico City's 114,000-seat Aztec Stadium, a structure as much a monument to the present civilization of Mexico as the pyramids of Teotihuacán are to the past. An estimated eight hundred million people—more people than watched the first Moon Walk—considered that World Cup Final the greatest show on earth.

Some of those people called it soccer. Many more called it football (for soccer's real name is Association Football) or *fútbol, voetbal, fussball,* or *fotbol.* But whatever it is called, the game's the same the world over. It is the sport out of which grew Rugby Football and plain American football.

1

A Moscow Dynamo player is surrounded by three Cosmos players. The Dynamos visited the United States in 1972.

The origin of soccer, as with so many other sports, is lost in antiquity. There have always been ball-type games, even back in early China. But, the first real form of soccer is *alleged* to have occurred when the ancient Britons chopped off the heads of invading Danes and kicked them around for fun.

Whether or not this is true, we do know that a recognizable form of soccer began in England in the nineteenth century. The players, with long droopy mustaches, and drawers that drooped even more, played, from what we can tell from old prints, rather like young boys play today: grouping around the ball, all rushing around in bunches together. While the technical movement of today was missing, there were solid goal posts with a crossbar (sometimes of string) and the game was, nonetheless, recognizable as modern soccer.

The first rules of soccer were established in London in 1863. Thanks to British immigrants, sailors, and merchants going around the world, the modern game was played in the many cities and ports where English industry was, or where British merchant ships called. For instance, the Moscow Dynamo team was originally formed by English industrialists who set up some cotton mills in Moscow and formed a soccer team for the workers which evolved into the present-day, world-famous Moscow Dynamo.

The great AC Milan team in Italy, many times Italian champions, was originally the Milan Cricket and Football Club, organized by a group of British businessmen to play cricket and football in Milan. In Argentina, one of the best known teams in South America, Banfield, was founded by an English concern called Banfield, Ltd. Thus, in the early 1900's the modern game of soccer was introduced round the world by the British. But in the 1920's and 1930's, several nations, having shed the trappings of the British influence, started to produce fine teams and great players. Actually, over the years the local inhabitants began to add touches and refinements to the game, and soon these differences in approach to soccer developed into distinct national styles. There is today an Italian style; a Brazilian style; a Hungarian, a German, and an English style. And so on.

Because of the tremendous growth through so many countries in the world, the Fédération Internationale de Football Association (FIFA) was formed to control the game world-wide. Presently, there are 146 nations belonging to the FIFA.

Each of the FIFA member countries has a national association, but every one except the English association has the name of the country added to its title for identification purposes. For example: the Scottish Football Association, the Federación Mexicana de Fútbol Asociación, the Deutscher Fussball-Bund, as the case may be. But The Football Association is, in fact, the English Association, which was, of course, the very first one. Incidentally, the word soccer is derived from association, first shortened to Assoc., then corrupted to soccer.

SOCCER IN THE UNITED STATES

Now, just as the nations of Europe and South America, of Africa and Asia and Oceania, of Central America and that part of North America which ends at the Mexican-United States border have done before us, we're establishing soccer *our* style—U.S. style and Canadian style. And for over fifty years, soccer has played a very minor role on the American sports scene. There was soccer in the United States, but apart from its popularity in the Ivy League and a few eastern colleges—the famous 1869 game between Princeton and Rutgers, which is claimed to be the start of intercollegiate football, was a game of soccer—it was played almost exclusively by recently arrived immigrants. During the 1920's a number of major corporations, including Bethlehem Steel, went to the trouble of importing some of Europe's top professional stars for the benefit of their recently immigrated workers.

Because of the lack of world communications, most of these imported players were unknown to the average American sports fan and soccer's only interest was with these new immigrants. Attendance at games in the 1920's and early 1930's was good: All of them were just really reliving their days in the lands they had just left, and soccer was a last cultural thread that new Americans had with their homelands. They carried on the game, as they did at home, in minority cliques, and with no regard for either American influence or American participation. As a result, their influence on the game was minimal. This was especially true since the second-generation American usually goes the opposite route: in casting aside the bonds of a foreign culture, he often includes the inheritance of soccer. To affirm his Americanism, he chooses to play a typically American sport in which he will receive considerable recognition: baseball, basketball, or football.

This situation continued until 1967, when the first real attempt was made to popularize soccer in America outside the ethnic circles and the rather limited school play. But the early problem of professional soccer in the United States was that before a ball was kicked there was a war between two leagues. We know that it is traditional in this country for two leagues to grow up and have battles with each other before they eventually merge. But in soccer, we started with a game that was not known to the American public and here were two leagues fighting for the right to attract a small number of spectators.

The National Professional Soccer League had a rich TV contract, while the United Soccer Association had the recognition of the governing body of the sport in this country, the United States Soccer Football Association, and in turn the recognition of the FIFA. In other words, the National Professional Soccer League, operated with lots of publicity but no international recognition. This meant that no overseas teams or foreign stars would play against or in the NPSL. If, however, the two leagues had combined their resources from the start, they would have had combined recognition—which would have made it easier to obtain players, practical to obtain foreign games, *and* given access to TV money. But they started off in a war, and it took twelve months of hard battling on both sides and tremendous losses in both leagues before they merged in January 1968 into the North American Soccer League. Of the twenty-one teams operating in two warring leagues, we ended up with seventeen teams operating in one merged legal and TV-contracted league.

The standard of play in these first two years was quite high; in fact, the North American Soccer League Clubs beat the champions of England twice and also won over several other foreign teams. Crowds in some cities were becoming very receptive. For instance, in 1967 nearly seventeen thousand paid to see the championship game between the Baltimore Bays (managed by Clive Toye) and the Oakland Clippers. There were also crowds of over twenty thousand to see NASL against the great Pele and the Santos of Brazil. In fact, two of our teams —the Cleveland Stokers and the New York Generals—beat the Santos. One of the reasons why the Generals won was that co-author Gordon Bradley had the job of shadowing Pele, the "King of Soccer." And he did it so effectively that Pele didn't score; the Santos fumbled along without the help of the world's greatest player and the Generals won the game.

But in spite of these bright spots, the losses were still piling up and there came a stark division of attitude between the managements of the NASL clubs. One group wanted to immediately move into the superstar category and spend a great deal of money buying foreign stars whose names were more easily recognizable—especially to the ethnic fans in major cities such as New York, Chicago, and Los Angeles. The other group, mainly from cities where soccer hadn't been known at all until the advent of the NASL, believed that the only way to operate was to spend the available money on the development of the game through the youth rather than bringing over foreign players and other so-called professionals.

The argument continued to the point where the League was almost dead, despite mounting interest and gradual signs of growth in the game. Finally, five teams who believed in the development of the game through the youth got together. And, in 1969, devoted almost three-quarters of their attention, time, and budget to the game in their own areas of the country. By 1971, the NASL had grown to eight teams. And, by the fall of 1972 it was in a very healthy state, with people seeing not only a fine standard of play on the field—good enough for Dallas to tie with the Moscow Dynamos and for New York to beat the Israeli champions, Maccabi–Tel-Aviv, 5–2—but an increasing number of fans in the stands.

The most encouraging factor is the enthusiasm of the native-born Americans and the increasing number of young people who are playing

The object of the game is to put the ball into the net. Here Everald Cummings (Number 20) puts one past the goalie.

the game. American boys from age six and up are playing soccer in typical community-oriented leagues across the country; their fathers and mothers are totally involved in organizing, running, and coaching these leagues. There is also a tremendous growth of soccer in high schools and colleges.

Why has soccer caught on in the United States to the point the press has called it "the fastest growing sport in America"? Soccer has gained impetus because it is a simple game. Simple in that it is easy to understand, easy to organize into leagues. The rules of the game are not difficult to follow. The equipment is inexpensive and minimal. All that is needed is a level field, a pair of shorts, a T-shirt, a ball, a pair of sneakers, and the game is on. And, any boy—or anyone, for that matter—can play.

The greatest player of the last decade is 5 feet 9 inches and 160 pounds of superb muscular coordination. He is Pele of Brazil, a boy from a poor home who is now worth more than any athlete past, present—and probably future. His estimated worth exceeds three million a year.

George Best of Northern Ireland, who promised to be as great a player as Pele in the next few years, until his problems off the field caused him to drop out of soccer for all of the 1972–1973 winter, is only 5 feet 6 inches and weighs 145 pounds. In fact, just one look at

Cosmos players look on as Barry Mahy (Number 2) makes an effort to clear the ball out of danger area.

a soccer team lined up before the game will tell you one very important thing about the sport: almost anyone can play. You'll see tall guys and short guys standing side by side, and heavy guys and skinny guys—and they all meet on equal terms. It may, for instance, be an advantage to be tall when it comes to jumping for head balls, but when the ball is on the ground, height is no advantage at all. For example, the Cosmos players defending the NASL Championship Cup in 1973 offer this contrast: Siggy Stritzl is 5 feet 6 inches and 144 pounds; Randy Horton is 6 feet 2 inches at 200 pounds. The lesson is obvious—any boy of any shape or size can play soccer, can enjoy soccer, and can progress in soccer according to his desire and ability. One thing that all the players do have in common, though, is that they are in top physical condition. Most of them will have to play the full ninety minutes of the game (under NASL rules, only two substitutes are allowed) and this means ninety minutes of almost constant movement. Soccer can be a ballet. It can be brutal; a clash of bodies; a war between minds. A game of vigor and skill.

THE GAME

Soccer is a simple game of continuous action and constantly changing possession of the ball. While it is a team sport, each player is, neverthe-

Sometimes soccer can be a clash of bodies.

less, clearly an individual with skills and style all his own. But the beauty of soccer from the spectators' point of view is that the action can be witnessed with interest without learning numerous complicated rules. Basically, if you know the idea is to get the ball into the opponents' net, and that it has to be done without using the hands, you're ready to watch the sport. In fact, soccer has only seventeen "laws" and the following is a simple condensation of them. (The complete *Official Laws of the Game* are given in Appendix B.)

LAW I: *The Field of Play.* The overall dimensions of the soccer field are 100 to 130 yards in length, and 50 to 100 yards in width. The length should in all cases exceed the width.

The other dimensions of a soccer field remain fixed, whatever the overall size of the field, and are shown in the illustration on page 203.

LAW II: *The Ball.* Its circumference should not be more than 28 inches and not less than 27 inches. (In contrast, a basketball is 29 inches in circumference; a volleyball is 26 inches.) The weight of the ball at the start of the game should not be more than 16 ounces nor less than 14 ounces. The same leather ball is used throughout the entire game unless a change is authorized by the referee. In North America, and some European countries, a black and white ball is used; other countries employ a plain white or tan-colored ball.

LAW III: *Number of Players.* Each team consists of eleven players, one of whom must be the goalkeeper. A maximum of two substitutes may be used in a game.

There is only one occasion when a team must play with fewer than eleven players. If a referee sends a player off the field for disciplinary reasons, the player may not return and he may not be replaced.

LAW IV: *Player Equipment.* Consists of a shirt, shorts, stockings, and boots. The goalkeeper must wear colors which distinguish him from the other players. Incidentally, the goalkeeper is the only player on the team who is allowed to use his hands. He can only do this within his own penalty area.

LAW V: *Referees.* One referee is appointed for each match. He is responsible for control of the game and his decisions are final.

LAW VI: *Linesmen.* Two linesmen assist the referee by indicating offside when the ball is out of play, and which team is entitled to the corner kick or throw-in.

LAW VII: *Duration of the Game.* Shall be two equal periods of 45 minutes unless otherwise agreed upon.

LAW VIII: *The Start of Play.* A flip of a coin decides which team will kick off. Each team must stay on its own half of the field and the defending players must be at least 10 yards from the ball until it is kicked.

After a goal, the team scored upon kicks off. After half-time, the teams change goals and the kick-off will be taken by the opposite team to that which started the game. A goal cannot be scored directly from a kick-off.

LAW IX: *Ball In and Out of Play.* The ball is out of play when (a) it has wholly crossed the goal line or touch line, whether on the ground or in the air; (b) when the game has been stopped by the referee.

LAW X: *Method of Scoring.* A goal is scored when the whole of the ball has passed over the goal line, between the goal posts and under the crossbar.

LAW XI: *Offside.* A player is offside if he is nearer his opponent's goal line than the ball at the moment the ball is played unless, (a) he is in his own half of the field of play, (b) there are two of his opponents nearer to their own goal line than he is, (c) the ball last touched an

The referee is in complete control
of the game. Here he indicates three
infractions: *(top)* handling of the ball;
(center) foot over sideline on throw-in;
and *(bottom)* pushing.

opponent or was last played by him, (d) he receives the ball direct from a goal kick, a corner kick, a throw-in, or when dropped by the referee.

LAW XII: *Fouls and Misconduct.* A player who intentionally attempts to or actually: (1) kicks (2) trips (3) jumps at (4) charges violently (5) charges from behind (6) strikes (7) holds or (8) pushes an opponent, or (9) intentionally handles the ball, shall be penalized by a direct free kick. Any one of these nine offenses intentionally committed in the penalty area by a defender will result in a penalty kick against the team that committed the foul.

A player committing less flagrant violations such as offside, dangerous plays, obstruction, or ungentlemanly conduct will be penalized by an indirect free kick.

LAW XIII: *Free Kicks.* Are classified into two categories: "Direct" (from which a goal can be scored directly by the kicker). "Indirect" (which must touch at least one other player before entering the goal.)

For all free kicks the offending team must be at least 10 yards from the ball until it is kicked.

The linesman at the left is indicating offside, while the one on right is pointing the flag in the direction a throw-in has to be taken.

A

B

The nine fouls of soccer: A) kicking an opponent; B) tripping; C) jumping at an opponent; D) violent charging; E) charging from behind; F) striking an opponent; G) holding an opponent; H) pushing an opponent; and I) intentionally handling the ball.

H

I

C

D

E

G

F

The soccer goalkeeper is the only player who can touch the ball on the field of play with his hands.

LAW XIV: *Penalty Kick.* A direct free kick taken at the penalty mark. All players except the player taking the kick and the goalkeeper must stay outside the penalty area and at least 10 yards from the ball (hence the arc at edge of penalty area).

LAW XV: *Throw-in.* When the ball has wholly crossed the touch line it is put back into play by a throw-in from the spot where it went out and by a player from the opposite team that last touched it. A goal cannot be scored directly from a throw-in.

LAW XVI: *Goal kick.* When the ball has wholly crossed the goal line after being last touched by a player from the attacking team, it is put back into play by a kick from the goal area by the defending team.

LAW XVII: *Corner Kick.* When the ball has wholly crossed the goal line after being last touched by a player from the defending team, it is put back into play by the attacking team with a kick from the corner on the side the ball went out.

So much for the rules of the game of soccer. Now let's take a look at the equipment and how the game is played.

The Equipment and Players

As described in Chapter 1, soccer is a simple game to follow, even for the first-time spectator. It is a flowing game. There is hard tackling— not of the American football type—but physical aggression between players who are trying to get the ball. There is enormous agility by the goalkeeper and by players kicking the ball out of the air, by players going up to head it to try and score or to stop goals. There is enormous technical skill in controlling the ball with any part of the body except the hands and arms. There is precision in the way a player in a split second can lay on an accurate pass from 5 to 50 yards, either to a teammate or into an open space where a teammate can run to gather the ball.

There is an enormous degree of tactical play which you can begin to appreciate after having seen just a couple of games. It is soon apparent that there is more going on than players running around and trying to kick the ball or head the ball to each other. The game can be as simple as that. Or it can be as complex as chess. Others have said it before: the more you know about soccer, the more you realize how little you do know. You can spend a lifetime watching soccer and still be learning, still be seeing another nuance in a run or in a pass or in a team's play.

SOCCER EQUIPMENT

Little equipment is needed for soccer. Shorts and jerseys, shoes, knee-length socks, and a ball are all one needs to play competitive soccer. A high school superintendent friend of ours recently stated that he could outfit an *entire* soccer team for the cost of equipping *one* football player. This economy in equipment is one of the reasons for the popularity of soccer in financially pressed schools.

The shoes are the most important part of a player's personal equipment. Much experimenting has been done to produce a shoe suited to individual needs, yet conforming to soccer regulations. The lightweight shoe is now much preferred to the more durable, heavy type. The shoe should fit like a glove and should be fastened around the sole and tied at the outer side. The rules limit the kinds of bars or studs (cleats) that can be used on the soles and heels and the distance they can project. Briefly, the shoe regulation states that all studs must be made of leather, soft rubber, aluminum-plastic, or similar material and must not project more than half an inch, or have any protruding nails or edges.

Some soccer leagues have a compulsory ruling that the players must wear numbers on the backs of shirts or jerseys, but this is not necessary for junior teams. The NASL insists on numbers front and back. Colors of jerseys and shorts should be distinguishable between the opposing sides, with the goalkeeper's jersey in a color distinguishable from both his own team and the opposition. This is done so that the referee can easily see the color of the jersey of the player handling the ball. In other words, the goalies stick out like sore thumbs from everybody else on the field.

Green, red, or black are the recognized international goalkeeper's colors. Since we are never sure what colors we may come up against in the opposing team, the Cosmos always have at least three different colors for our goalkeeper. While our 1972 goalie, Richie Blackmore, prefers blue, if we come up against a blue-clad team, he will change into green if we are wearing our yellow jerseys, or, if we are wearing our green uniforms, into yellow. (The NASL home team always has first choice of uniform color.) If the necessary contrast is still not obtained, Blackmore will go to black. Incidentally, many goalkeepers fancy themselves in black because Lev Yashin's theory is that black acts as a kind of magnet for a player's attention. That is, when a player is just about ready to shoot on goal, the all-black uniform somehow attracts his attention and tends, subconsciously, to drag the ball towards the goalkeeper. (Russia's Yashin was considered the world's greatest goalkeeper until his retirement in 1971.)

To protect their elbows in a dive, most goaltenders wear long-sleeved jerseys. Goalkeepers will also sometimes wear a light pair of gloves to help them catch the ball and hold it. This is especially true in wet or cold weather. These gloves have stippled surfaces—small raised spots

The goalkeeper wears a different color uniform than the other players on the field. Some goalies like to wear goalkeeping gloves, particularly on wet days, but the majority won't do so under normal playing conditions.

—that help the ball to cling to them. A few goalkeepers wear caps to protect their eyes against the sun.

If you wear glasses, be sure to wear the contact type or use sport frames and a good band to hold them in place. We have known fine players with glasses who make some of the best head shots in the game, although no player has reached the top class without switching from glasses to contact lenses.

Some players use light shin guards tucked inside their socks for protection against injury. The majority, however, seem to prefer running the risk of a scraped shin to that of carrying any extra weight. An athletic support of the cup-in-pouch style is an almost mandatory piece of equipment.

A player is not allowed to wear anything such as a watch or ring which may cause injury to another player. If a player is found to have any article of uniform or personal equipment not conforming to established regulations, he is sent off the field. And he can't return without first reporting to the referee, who must satisfy himself that the player's uniform is in order. The player can only enter the game when the ball has ceased to be in play.

PLAYERS AND THEIR POSITIONS ON THE TEAM

Before discussing techniques and tactics in detail, we think that it's a good idea to describe briefly the actual functions of the various positions in the team. Each player must know what is expected of him, and he must also know what to expect of his teammates. In fact, the relative freedom of the game, the way in which players change positions all the time, leaves many first-time spectators somewhat bewildered. "But what about the plays?" they ask. "Aren't there any set plays?" To which the answer is: very few.

During the game the players must always be on the alert to adjust to the action that changes almost every second. Imagine a player making a short run—say about 10 yards—with the ball. During this run he may change direction two or three times, or he may fake to change direction; he may fake to make a pass to his left, or his right, or straight ahead; he may suddenly accelerate or slow down. Every one of these moves—even a subtle one like a slight movement of the head to look in one direction—must be caught by the opposing players and acted on immediately: either dismissed as a fake, or matched by a counter-move. Similarly, the player's own teammates must respond to his action by running into positions to receive a pass, or to support him if he runs into trouble. Clearly, then, in a soccer game a great deal goes on, and to really appreciate the intricacies of the sport the spectator must learn to widen his vision so that he is watching not only the player with the ball, but the players off the ball, too.

While set plays are not a part of soccer action, there are certain formations that the whole team uses as a loose basis for their positional play. To simplify matters, there are four types of soccer players: (1) goalkeepers, (2) defenders, or fullbacks, (3) midfield players, or linkmen, and (4) attackers, or forwards, or strikers. The skill and knowledge with which each player performs his function determines the whole balance of the team and its combination as an effective force either in attack or defense.

Each team, of course, has a goalkeeper. But, the exact number of defenders, linkmen, and forwards depends on the system of play employed by the coach. As described in Chapter 6, the purpose of a system of play is to spell out to players their major responsibilities in terms of attack and defense while still allowing for individualism, initiative and inventiveness. Our Cosmos team primarily uses a 4-2-4 system. That means that we generally play four defenders, two linkmen, and four attackers. (In describing the tactical formations, the position of the goalkeeper is omitted—he is always in the same position on every team.) On occasions we may switch to 4-3-3, which means that we have four defenders, three midfield players, and three forwards.

The formation indicates only the *main* responsibility of each player. But everyone must be prepared to play another's position, even if only for a second or two. We'll take a further look at systems of play later in the book, but for now let's find out what the duties are of each of the four types of soccer players.

THE GOALKEEPER

The goalkeeper's primary task is guarding his team's goal. He is the last line of defense. When he is beaten, the goal is at the mercy of the opposing forwards. That is, it could be that every time he makes a mistake he gives away a goal; therefore, the goalkeeper must keep in mind that safety is his first consideration.

The goalkeeper also has an important function in the attack. Not only is he the last line of defense, he is also the first stage of the attack. From his every clearance, an attacking movement should be started. If he kicks or throws the ball to an opponent he is wasting his teammate's time and probably increasing his own work. We well remember the Cosmos' second goal in our 5-2 win over the Israeli Champions Maccabi–Tel-Aviv in 1972. Richie Blackmore, our goalkeeper, threw an accurate 25-yard pass to midfielder John Kerr. Kerr ran with the ball maybe 10 yards before a "give and go" with Roby Young, and one pass later Randy Horton was scoring the second of his three goals in a move begun by Blackmore's alertness and accuracy.

Because a goalkeeper's decisions can be vital to the outcome of the game, the good goalie must possess qualities of leadership. Actually, many of his specialized abilities, such as fielding the ball, and diving for the ball at full stretch, are unrelated to those required in the other positions on the team. Full details on the techniques of goalkeeping are given in Chapter 5.

DEFENSE

Defending is the responsibility of every player on the team. However, the method and degree of responsibility varies from position to position. When a team loses possession of the ball to the opponents, its players must immediately make it as difficult as possible for individual opponents to pass or receive the ball by intelligent positioning and

The goalkeeper is "in the thick of it" when the ball is at his end of the field. Here the goalie jumps to punch the ball clear in a dangerous scoring situation.

anticipation. But the players whose prime concern lies with the defense are the fullbacks or backs.

In modern soccer systems there is invariably a back line of four defensive players—two center-backs, a right-back and a left-back. The right- and left-backs have as their primary individual task the prevention of attacks along the wings.

The first form of prevention is to anticipate an offense, and intercept a pass before it can reach its target. The second is to tackle and dispossess the immediate opponent on the wing, and if attempts to get possession fail, the back must jockey the opponent and steer him down the touchline and away from the goal. For instance, the right-back plays on the inside of the opposing left wing or outside forward so as to force him towards the sideline and prevent him cutting in towards the middle. If the outside-left forward evades him down the flank, there is still a chance for him to run towards the goal and help as the outside man is moving in towards goal.

The outside defensive back—either left or right—can't always be concerned with just his immediate opponent. When the ball is on the

Being able to execute a good clearance under close conditions is a must for the defense backs.

other flank, he must drop back and move infield to cover his teammate. His center-fullback (formerly called the center-halfback) may be taken out to the far wing by the opposing striker. The left- or right-backs must then cover the center of the field to block any breakthrough by the attackers.

The sideline, which is of value to him in restricting the movements of the opposing outside forward, becomes a problem when the outside defensive back obtains possession of the ball himself. A great deal of his kicking is performed and directed close to the sideline and requires very careful judgment. Power in his kick is most important for a full-back, but the defender who boots the ball haphazardly upfield is no help to his teammates. The linkmen and forwards can stage a better attack on goal if they are given possession of the ball on their half of the field than if they have to scramble for it in their opponents' half.

The center-fullback (there may be one or two, depending on the team's system of play) should use his central position to exert a steady-ing influence on the entire defense unit. He is the pivot, forever on the alert, his judgment continually being tested. Should he move across to

Fullbacks—such as the Cosmos' Werner Roth (Number 4)—must be able to move up the field to start an attack.

tackle that striker? Should he attempt to intercept that pass, or can he withdraw and gain time for his teammate to cover up? Will the goal-keeper come out for a ball? He is constantly assessing the various possibilities of the game and the capabilities of the players, and is frequently looked upon as the most suitable player to captain a team or later become a coach. It was into the demanding position of center-half that we, in 1972, put one of the most promising young American players—Werner Roth—with outstanding results.

The fullback's job isn't completed when he has dispossessed an attacking opponent; this is only the beginning of his duties. His next thought must be how best he can serve on attack. He must, in fact, think all the time of how he can fit his largely defensive role into the wider scheme of the team's attack. Also, the center-fullback who does no more than shadow the opposing striker around the field is not doing his full job. Like the goalkeeper and the backs, he, too, has a function in attack. In other words, when a team is on the defensive, the whole team is on the defensive; and when the team is on the offensive, the entire team must be on the offensive. For example, in one game last year, the St. Louis Stars tied us 3-3: the fullbacks were the ones who either scored or assisted in all three goals.

LINKMEN

The fundamental qualities of a midfield player (linkman) are endurance, shrewd anticipation, quick tackling moves, and excellent ball-handling ability. The midfield player is often referred to as the "engine room" personnel of the team and is usually the fiery, energetic, skillful player. On a modern soccer team there are generally two to three linkmen (formerly known as halves or halfbacks under old soccer terminology) on the field. The midfield player usually covers the opposing linkman, but he must also control the midfield. It's a proven fact that the team that controls this area generally wins the game.

The midfield player is the connecting link between the defense and the forwards. Much depends upon his ability to serve the ball accurately and intelligently (i.e., the depth of the penetration of the attack). Working from defense to attack and from attack to defense, he is constantly on the move. Often the linkman is the most overworked member of the team. He must possess outstanding ball-handling skills. He must be in top physical condition. The linkman has to control the play of the game, breaking opponents' attacks in their early stages, and setting up and carrying through his own team's attacks. The midfield player must be adept at working his way out of "smothered" conditions, often starting with his back towards the opponents' goal. Generally, he's not only in at the start of these moves—he is also in at the kill, ready to shoot with the forwards should the opportunity present itself.

The linkman should always be present in the zone of immediate play or, at least, on the fringe of it. He assists on corners in defense as well as in attack, he participates in practically every throw-in on his side of the field, and is nearby for every throw-in on the other side of the field. But above all, the linkman must be a sound thinker, for he is the prime tactician in the team.

THE ATTACKERS

In modern soccer, there are two special types of attackers: the outside forwards and the strikers. There are two outside forwards—outside-right and outside-left. And there are from one to two, depending on system of play, strikers on the attacking line.

The striker is probably valued more for his goal-scoring achievements than for anything else. He is more centrally positioned for scoring than

Linkmen such as the Cosmos' Dieter Zajdel (Number 22) must be able to control the ball *(above)* or tackle for it *(right)*.

the two outside forwards. True, he must have the "goal getting" abilities of shooting and heading with accuracy and power; but the better player the striker is, the more closely will he be covered by the opposing defense. Actually, because of this close coverage, a striker is apt to meet with many failures. He will rarely receive the ball in ideal circumstances: too often it will come to him with his back to the goal and a center-back on his heels. However, he must reverse his strategy by putting a short pass back to a linkman, lobbing the ball sideways out to the outside forwards, or even turning with it in an attempt to dribble past the center-back.

A good striker frequently can use close coverage to his advantage. He has the opportunity to lure defenders into false positions, to take them away from the middle of the field and leave the central path to the goal open for his teammates. Thus, he is not only the spearhead of the attack, but also can be the pivot around which the attack revolves. A top-notch striker is never a selfish player.

The outside forward must have speed. Many of the linking movements between the midfield players and strikers end with a dash by the outside forward winger for a ball placed just behind the opposing

defense. And his advanced position upfield often means that if he passes the opposing fullback he is alone, with only his speed to help him make a direct attack on goal. He must have good ball control and dribbling skill. With the out-of-bounds line on one side of him and the opposing fullback on the other, the outside forward has little room to move. If he is a clever dribbler, he can frequently draw the defense in around him, and thus weaken their coverage in front of the goal. But he must know when to release the ball, and his centering passes must be properly timed and accurate.

With good outside play, a team can attack on a broad front, switching the thrust from one side to the other, thus upsetting the balance of the defense. Without effective outside play the attack is forced into a narrow channel down the center of the field, giving the defense an easy task of stifling it. In other words, fast, skillful outside forwards will not only weaken the defense but will keep it on the run.

As described in Chapter 6, team formation or systems of play vary. In addition, the duties of the players may change slightly. But in most cases, when a team is in possession of the ball it is on the attack; when it loses the ball it is on the defense. Or as we say on the Cosmos, "The

The ability to head a ball on net is a very important qualification of a striker.

moment that we lose possession of the ball, the whole team thinks defensively, but the instant we gain possession of it, the entire team thinks offensively."

This rapid change of role, of course, means that players keep within range of each other. When the attack presses forward, the defense must also move upfield. When the defense is forced back, the attack must also fall back. If the gap between the defense and attack becomes too wide, they will lose contact with each other, linking will become much more difficult, and accurate passing impossible. We have seen that, although each player has a principal function in attack or defense, neither is exclusive to any player. But the rapid interchange between defense and attack places the lion's share of work on the linking players. It is from them that the team acquires its cohesion.

SUMMATION

Every defender—even the goalkeeper—must play a part in stimulating intelligent attacking moves. As we stated earlier in this chapter, the goalkeeper can do it by clearing the ball with accurate low throws or kicks. The backs can do it by well-judged low passing rather than

Cosmos' striker, Randy Horton, is back on defense, helping out.

sky-high clearance kicks. There may be some occasions when it is wise to clear the ball with a hefty kick upfield, but most of the time it's more essential that the transition from defense to attack is made anything but a scramble for a loose ball. The forwards, of course, have their part to play in defense. And the attackers can play a major part in helping to regain possession. Every player on the field must be prepared to adapt his play—or even his role—to the needs of the various situations that may arise during the game. Remember that no player in a team game should ever say, "That's not my job."

The Basic Technique
of Soccer: Kicking

SOCCER has often been called the game of a *foot* and of a *ball*. Therefore, to be a soccer player you must be able to kick a ball properly.

Kicking in soccer is any action taken in which the foot strikes the ball. In other words, any time your foot comes in contact with the soccer ball, you're kicking. In playing the game, kicking serves three major functions: shooting, passing, and clearing of a ball. Let's take a brief look at the three basic uses of kicking:

1. *Shooting*   As described in Chapter 7, scoring is the object of soccer and to score you must be able to shoot. Any of the kicks mentioned in this chapter can be used to put the ball into the net, but the low drive described on page 32 is the most effective. It's not the speed of the ball or how hard it is kicked, it's how accurate the shot is that puts the ball behind the goalkeeper. If you have, of course, a hard, accurate shot, like the Cosmos' Josef Jelinek and Jorge Siega, so much the better.

2. *Passing*   It's often stated that if a player can't pass the ball he can't play the game. What should be said, of course, is that if you can't pass the ball accurately it is unlikely that you'll be effective in the higher levels of soccer. Good passing requires both accuracy and good judgment. Before the kick begins, you should assess the location of your pass receiver; his speed; direction of movement; the space and the disposition of opposing players. From the commencement of the kick, you must concentrate on developing the right amount of power and making accurate contact with the ball. This means that your eyes are fixed firmly on the ball during the actual kicking motion and they remain focused on the same place even after the ball has gone.

3. *Clearing of a Ball*   Many times in the defensive play of soccer

Looks like an unusual kick is coming!

(see Chapter 8), it is very important to quickly get the ball out of the territory you're defending. A long power kick is the best method. When clearing the ball, power and length of kick are important factors.

WHAT IS A SOCCER KICK?

Practically any part of the surface of the foot can be employed in kicking the ball. The sole of the foot is used to push a bouncing ball to a nearby player; the heel is used to send the ball backwards; the inside and outside of the feet are used in passing; the instep is used for drives, lofting, volleys, and half-volleys. Even the toe of the shoe is used to prod the ball along when it is too far out of reach to do anything else. But while there are several different ways of kicking a soccer ball, over 90 per cent are done with the inside-of-foot or the instep. The latter is the so-called "soccer-style" kick that has revolutionized football. The instep kick is the one used by such professional football stars as Jan Stenerud, Pete Gogolak, Garo Ypremian, and Bobby Howfield. Incidentally, Howfield of the New York Jets and Gordon Bradley played soccer against one another in England.

A typical soccer
kick is performed by
two Cosmos players.

The soccer-style kick provides for accuracy that is virtually impossible to achieve with the "old-fashioned" toe-kicking method. Kicking with the toes gives only a small area of contact with the ball—be it a soccer ball or football. But when the whole of the instep is "wrapped" around the ball, a large area of contact is made, and because the foot is already well braced, very strong kicking power can be applied.

Incidentally, a soccer ball may be kicked on the ground or in the air, and an all-around good player must know how to execute each one of them.

INSTEP KICKS

There are two basic types of instep kicks: the low drive and the lofted kick. While with both types individual player technique may vary a little, the instep kick is made by turning your kicking foot slightly outward so that the ball makes contact with the inside part of the instep where the shoe is laced. Use the curve of your ankle joint to literally "wrap" itself around the curve of the ball. On impact, your foot actually sinks into the ball so that a large surface area of your foot meets a large surface area of the ball. It's important to keep in mind that power from this kick is obtained from the muscles of your knee, not from the muscles of your hip. Thus, if you concentrate on the lower part of your leg and firm it before making contact with the ball, you will kick well and be able to control direction.

The Low Drive   The key to this type of instep kick is the way in which the instep makes contact with the ball. Your toes must be kept well down so that your instep drives the ball low to the ground or along it. The position of your knee in relation to the ball is also important. If your knee is too far forward, your instep will be driving down and the force of the kick will be expended in driving the ball down into the ground. If your knee is too far behind the ball, your instep will be on the upward swing and the ball will be lifted well off the ground. To bring your kicking knee properly over the ball, your hips should also be over your kicking foot at the moment of contact. Therefore, your standing foot should be placed alongside the ball—anywhere from 4 to 12 inches away. Your toe shouldn't move too far in front of the ball or much behind it if the kick is to be strong and the ball kept low.

When approaching the ball in line with the direction of the kick, you should time your stride—gathering pace as you near the ball—to bring your non-kicking foot down, heel first, alongside the ball. Your knee should be slightly bent. The body should move forward until

(top) The foot is coming into contact with the ball. Note how the player is looking down with his upper body over the ball. *(center)* A "close-up" before the foot makes contact. Because of the side approach the part of the foot which will strike the ball first will be the eyelets on the left side of the shoe. *(bottom)* The actual contact of the foot.

The close-up position for the full instep kick. The ball is kicked with the center of the instep.

almost vertical over the ball. At this time your shoulders are bent slightly forward and your head should be looking down. Your kicking leg should be extended at the hip joint and flexed at the knee joint in typical running action. As your kicking leg swings through, your shoulders and arms begin to twist in the opposite direction. Your kicking knee passes over the ball and your foot is braced with toe downwards. When your knee completes its extension and the ball is driven away, your kicking leg continues its swing forward and upward, while your body rises up on the toes of your standing leg. The arm opposite to your kicking foot completes its counterswing across the body. The whole motion is coordinated to give pace and strength to the kick at the precise moment of contact.

The head should be kept down until the kick has been made. Size up the target before or during your approach run. But at the moment of kicking concentrate on the ball. All too frequently, beginning players, anxious to see the result of their kick, tend to throw the head back before the kick has been completed.

If the opportunity presents itself, most soccer players prefer to approach the ball at an angle. For instance, if you're kicking the ball with your right foot, the line of your run may be between 20 and 50 degrees to the left of the target line. Your standing foot is still placed parallel to the line of the kick by turning it outwards. This enables your right hip to swing round into action. If the run up is rather fast, you can

(left) Approaching the ball from the side for an instep lofted kick. *(right)* The completed follow-through.

check your angled impetus by leaning slightly to the left as the standing foot goes down alongside the ball. The pendulum swing of your kicking foot is slightly inclined, but it still sweeps through the center of the ball.

The Lofted Kick   To loft a ground ball into the air, your foot must make contact well below the center of the ball: your toe must swing under the ball and your instep lifted upward as contact is made. Of course, your toe can be held directly downwards, or turned downwards and inwards, but your hip, which is the fulcrum of the leg swing, must be behind the ball to lift it effectively. Your standing foot should be placed slightly to the side (5 to 10 inches) and behind the ball. With such a stance, the trunk of your body must lean backwards to reach the ball. Your hips can be kept back by folding at the waist, but this reduces the power of the kick.

If the approach is made from the side, your kicking leg should sweep round to bring your foot obliquely under the ball in a scooping action. In this case, your standing foot is placed some 8 to 15 inches to the side of the ball. Your weight should be on your standing foot, which is well bent at the knee. If the kick is powerful, your follow-through swings the kicking leg well across the body.

When too much height and not enough distance or "carry" is obtained, your foot is being applied too far under the ball during impact. This means that the ball has been directed upwards, and horizontal force is being wasted. When you find that you're pulling your long kicks

(above) Close up of inside of foot kick or pass showing the ball coming into contact above the arch of the foot. The standing or non-kicking foot is positioned alongside the ball. *(right)* Completion of the inside of the foot pass. Note that the kicking foot is positioned at right angles to the body.

to one side or the other, you can often adjust by slightly exaggerating the degree that your shoulder, corresponding to your non-kicking foot, points and remains pointing in the direction of the target or receiving player.

The Instep Kick on the Turn   In most instances, a sideways approach to the ball requires only a slight body turn during the kicking motion. But there may be occasions when it's necessary to turn completely around to kick the ball in the desired direction. To achieve this, your standing foot, in the last stride, is angled as far as possible and placed alongside the ball. Your body can then complete the turn, and, pivoting on the ball of your foot, you can bring it into the normal position for a low drive. You'll usually veer out to the side of the ball in order to make the last stride from a sideways angle. If running fairly fast, you can stop your forward body motion by leaning slightly backwards as the last stride is made and placing your standing foot firmly into the ground. If the ball is rolling away from you, plant your standing foot down ahead of the ball so that it will be alongside your foot when the kick is made.

To loft a ball on the turn, your standing foot should be slightly behind the ball when the pivot is completed. The quick run and the power of the kick and its follow-through often compel you to fall backwards. You can usually prevent this by folding at your hips; however, if you do fall, you can then sit down and roll backwards.

Inside-of-the-Foot Kick   Whenever accuracy is more important than distance, this type of kick is employed. Actually the inside-of-the-foot kick is the easiest and most reliable way of sending the ball along. It is also the most popular way of passing.

The inside-of-the-foot kick is accomplished by turning the foot outward so that the inside of your shoe makes full contact with the ball, the sole of your shoe clearing the ground by an inch or so. Your standing foot is placed sufficiently to the side to allow your kicking leg a free swing. Both your knees should be kept slightly flexed and the weight is shifted more to the heel of your standing foot. It's not possible to apply a great deal of strength to the kick, for the range and power of the leg action is limited, but if the foot is applied crisply to the ball —more in the form of a stab than a loose swing—distances up to 35 yards can be achieved. But to keep the ball on the ground, remember that the line of force must be through the midline of the ball or above it. If the point of impact falls below the midline, the greater the likelihood of the ball being lifted. To make such an impact possible, your foot should be at the lowest point of its swing as impact is made. This is facilitated when your knee is over the ball. The further you are behind the ball, the more your foot will tend to swing upwards. Similarly, if you're too far over the ball, your foot will tend to be on the downswing; consequently, your foot will tend to force the ball into and off the ground.

The Chipped Kick   The term "chipped" is used to describe a kick in which the foot is employed under the ball in much the same manner as a golf club is used to make a chip shot. This kick is used to make the ball rise steeply into the air—it should clear an opponent who may be standing as close as 6 yards away. It's not a powerful kick, and the ball shouldn't rise too high in the air—approximately 10 feet off the ground is usually sufficient. When a chipped ball lands, it should stop almost immediately. This kick is used in both passing and shooting situations.

There are two basic methods of chipping a ball. In the first, the full instep is used and, to gain maximum height, the impact between the instep and ball is made on the underside of the ball. To accomplish this, the toe of your kicking foot is stabbed beneath the ball and into the ground (under soft ground conditions), digging up a piece of turf in the process. Don't extend your ankle a great deal, but hold it firm. Because of the natural curve between your ankle and instep, and since contact is at the lowest possible point of the ball's surface, the line of force is much nearer to the vertical than the horizontal. The ball is caused to

How a chipped
kick is executed.

spin backwards during the flight. This helps the ball to obtain height and, on landing, to stop rather than to roll. The speed of your kicking foot is developed almost entirely by a quick straightening of your knee, which isn't completed until after the ball has left. The approach run is almost in line with the intended direction of the kick. Your non-kicking foot is close to and level with the ball and there is little, if any, follow-through. Accuracy of contact is vital in this technique and your head should be kept down throughout the motion. When the ball is rolling in the direction of a planned chipped kick, the ball's motion allows you to get your kicking foot directly under the ball. It is most difficult to chip a pass when the ball is rolling away from you or when the ground is extremely hard.

The second chipping method involves an angled approach to the ball. The toe of your foot is outward and away from the direction of the intended line of flight of the ball as it's kicked. This means that the lower part of your instep and the upper part of the toe of your shoe are the only parts of your foot to make contact with the undersurface of the ball. In this style of chipped kick, your foot is swept rather than stabbed under the ball. The purpose of both chipped-kick techniques is to reduce horizontal force and make contact as far beneath the ball as possible.

The Banana or Swerve-Ball Kick   The ability to kick the ball so that it swerves is a most useful technique. In fact, as described later in the book, it was our Siggy Stritzl's ability to execute the "banana kick" that led to the New York Cosmos' first home victory in the North American Soccer League.

Let's take the low drive as an example of the principles involved in swerving a ball on the ground. In this kick, you'll remember, contact is made at the center of the ball. This causes the ball to travel straight and low. If, however, you should make contact with the ball slightly left of center, as you stand facing it, the ball begins to spin in a clockwise direction. If you strike the ball to the right of the center, the ball spins in the opposite, or counterclockwise direction. In other words, the ball swerves in the direction of spin.

There are two varieties of the banana kick that can be employed. If you want to swerve the ball from left to right, wrap your instep around the left side of the ball as contact is made, or, to swerve the ball from right to left, turn your ankle inward so that contact is made by a part of the instep and part of the toe area of your foot. Contact is made on the outer side of the ball and your foot is swung vigorously across your

When making an outside-of-the-foot kick, the
first part of the foot to make contact with the ball
is the top of the small toe.

body and, therefore, across the ball. The approach run for such a
swerved kick tends to be much more in line with the ball and the target
than for most of the previous kicking techniques described.

To obtain identical results in the air (e.g., for a corner kick), contact
between your foot and the ball should take place below the horizontal
midline of the ball, depending on the amount of height desired.
Remember that the spin which causes a ball to swerve in the air also
causes a reversal of direction when the ball hits the ground. Goalkeepers are often tricked by a high swerving shot which lands in front of
them. Swerve causes the ball to move in one direction through the air
while spin causes the ball to move in the opposite direction off the
ground.

THE OUTSIDE-OF-THE-FOOT KICK

There are occasions when you don't have time to run around the ball
and kick with the inside of your foot or your instep. In such cases you
must use a side kick. While these kicks are lacking in power, they are
very useful for quick and deceptive passing, because the ball can be
flicked away in what appears to be a normal running stride. In such
an instance, you deliberately stand to one side of the ball—at a 90
degree angle to the way you're running. Then kick or push the front
outside edge of your foot at the ball with a whip-like motion of your
leg. Your knee will lead, followed by your ankle, and the rest of your
foot, each straightening in quick succession. Since it's very difficult to

Two different ways of back-heeling the ball. This type of kick or pass is generally used for short distances. Perfect timing is needed to produce an accurate pass.

position your knee over the ball in this technique, it is of the utmost importance that the point of impact is correct. In fact, most players, when making this pass, put a top spin on the ball since their foot tends to pass from the midline upwards while contact is being made.

In performing this outside-of-the-foot kick when running, your body weight is often immediately transferred to your kicking leg after contact with the ball has been made. This makes the kick into almost a side-step. You can place your standing foot slightly ahead of the ball and swing your lower leg outward at the ball as you complete your next stride. This is really a "dragging" action, and is most effective when playing the ball sideways. It's also possible to perform this outside pass by giving a short jab instead of a leg swing. This is handy when trying to avoid a tackle or when running at top speed. For a very short pass, you can actually "kick" the ball by placing the foot alongside it and then rotating your foot quickly outwards.

OTHER KICKS

There are a variety of short ground kicks—used primarily in passing situations—that are executed by experienced soccer players to get specific effects. Three of these kicks are performed as follows:

The Backheel Kick   To perform a backheel kick, you must allow your kicking foot to pass over the ball, then flex your knee to make a backward scooping motion. Your standing foot should be alongside the ball for your heel to gain some impetus before making contact. If you

The stretch-toe kick or pass can be used to advantage.

are running after the ball, stride ahead of it with your non-kicking foot, turning your kicking foot inward so that the ball makes contact more on the side of your foot. You can direct the ball obliquely backwards behind your standing leg. Similarly, you can move the ball diagonally backwards away from your body by turning your foot outward.

Another form of backheel is made by crossing your kicking foot outside the standing foot. But don't become so obsessed with tricks like backheeling that you over-use them in the game. Backheeling may deceive an opponent, but its unexpectedness may also deceive your teammate.

The Deflection Kick Sometimes the speed of the ball as it approaches you is sufficient to permit you to use your foot to divert it off course. In other words, the ball is allowed to "bounce" or "skid" off the foot. Attackers frequently employ this action to fake or "deke" a player or players out of position. That is, you can pretend to drive the ball but, in effect, stop your foot and merely deflect the ball to a nearby teammate.

The Jab Kick The smooth action of the jab makes it a most

The point of contact on an instep volley kick.

effective kick. When running, the quick jabbing action permits you to move the ball without stopping your running motion. The jabbing motion is produced by slightly withdrawing your foot as soon as contact with the ball is made. When in close challenging position with a tackling opponent, this quick jab action prevents your foot from being jammed into the tackle or from kicking some other player during your follow-through.

VOLLEY KICKING

The volleyed kick is made while the ball is in the air. The principles involved are basically the same as those for ground balls, except that your timing must be more accurate.

Long Volley Kick　When making a long volley kick, such as a defensive clearance, you should wait until the ball is near to the ground. This allows you to develop your leg swing in much the same manner as you do for the long lofted kick from ground level. Since the ball is off the ground, you'll have to lean slightly away from it (in both a backwards and a sideways direction) as you swing your leg. The higher the ball is when the volley kick is tried, the more you'll have to lean away from it. Swing your foot in the direction in which you desire the ball to travel. If the target, the path of the moving ball, and you are in line, the higher the ball will tend to travel. Actually, the height at which the ball is contacted will determine the amount of power.

The so-called ideal height for a deep volley kick is at about knee level. That is, as the ball comes to you, your standing foot is firmly planted and you swing your kicking leg from the thigh. When the ball is knee height—the knee of your kicking foot, of course, is not over the ball —kick with your full instep. As contact is made, lean your body backward, spreading your arms wide for balance, and rise up on the toes of the standing foot. You must use whatever power is available by swinging your kicking foot from the knee. Of course, the higher the ball, the greater the difficulty in stretching your ankle so that the ball is hit with the full instep. Most players on the Cosmos employ the leaning away, or falling, technique when volleying. This allows the kick to be made early, and with a maximum amount of power. The direction of the body lean is, roughly speaking, at right angles to the path of the ball and the direction in which it is intended to travel. Leaning away from the ball permits your kicking leg to be lifted to a height which is as near to being level with the ball as possible. This in itself permits a ball to be kicked with a lower trajectory and is important when shooting on goal.

When volleying a low ball (between the ankle and knee height) for power, you should keep your toes pointed down and should strike with the full instep. Be sure to kick the ball with a sharp knee movement without making too great a follow-through. Your body and head should be kept leaning forward.

The Short Volley   The short volley—frequently used in passing situations—is similar to the long volley except that very little full leg swing is employed, and the motion is brought about by using your lower leg almost exclusively. This allows a pass to be made over either a very short distance or a fairly long one, because the swinging action at your knee joint is natural and free. Balance is important in this technique because the position and stability of your standing leg provides the basis from which the short volley can be accomplished. The use of this short lever, from your knee downward, allows you to exercise a great deal of control, which is the foundation of accuracy.

The short volley can also be executed with the inside of the foot by turning sideways in the direction of the kick. A pass made in this way is rather limited and the technique is primarily used for short passing to a nearby teammate. The pass is achieved by a short swing

Two variations of Johnny Kerr (Number 6) clearance kick.

of your thigh caused by pivoting your hips. Your knee should usually be bent at right angles and held firm. The same is true of your ankle. This position permits the largest and flattest striking area of your foot and ankle to be employed.

The short volleyed kick can also be made by flicking the ball away, employing the outside of the foot. This technique is almost identical with that of the outside-of-the-foot kick described on page 40, except that almost all the movement comes from your ankle and knee.

The Half-Volley Kick   The half-volley is executed as the ball touches the ground. It requires a fine sense of timing. You must be able to bring the ball firmly into contact with your instep just at the proper moment of rebound. If made too soon, the ball will be volleyed high or may strike the end of the toe. If made late, the ball will have bounced too high and contact will be made, if at all, by the ankle or the shin.

The position of your body and the action of your leg to drive the ball low on the half-volley are basically the same as in making a low drive at a stationary ball. To loft the ball on the half-volley, the position and action are similar to those of the loft kick at a stationary ball. In both cases, the major difference is in the timing: that is, all surfaces of your foot can be used and whether or not the ball remains on the ground or in the air depends upon whether you follow the principles of ground passing technique or the principles of lofted passing technique described earlier in this chapter.

One of the most effective uses of a half-volley kick that all linkmen employ occurs when you have to deal with a ball which approaches you in the air and from which you wish to give a ground pass to a teammate without having to stop the ball. In making such a pass your contact with the ball must be most accurate, since the slightest error will produce a miskick. You must be well over the ball in a position which will enable you to watch the ball onto the ground. The kicking motion involves a fairly relaxed sweeping movement of your toe; foot and leg contact is made slightly above the midline of the ball to ensure that the ball is kept low.

The Overhead Volley or Scissors Kick   Volleying a ball backwards or over your head can be an effective technique for a surprise shot when any other attempt would require too much time.

To volley the ball behind you isn't hard to accomplish as long as you can lift it in an arch over your head. Contact with the ball in most instances is made at about waist level or a little higher, and the basic technique is the same as the long volley kick, except that the toes,

A demonstration
of a mid-air
backward
volley kick.

The scissors kick is probably the most exciting, but most difficult kick in soccer.

A skillfully made overhead volley clearance kick.

rather than being pointed out, are pulled back, making the ankle joint into a right angle that directs the ball backward. But remember, when volleying a ball backward, to be sure to get the top part of your body out of the path of the ball. This can be done only by falling backward as you throw your legs up into the air to kick the ball. That is, your body leans fully backward in the direction in which the ball is intended to be kicked. As your body falls backward, your hips may be raised if a powerful overhead kick is required. The lower your hips the less the amount of kicking power available.

A really powerful overhead kick, for instance when shooting, may involve a mid-air kick after a jump. The jump enables your kicking leg to be as high as the ball at the moment of impact—which means that the ball has a low trajectory. This type of overhead kick is often best executed when the ball is kicked backward over your shoulder by the opposite leg. In a right-foot shot, for example, you would use your right leg to kick the ball over your left shoulder. In actual play, the scissors kick must be used with caution. High kicking, when other players are nearby, is considered dangerous.

Ball Control and Other Soccer Basics

To play soccer you must, in addition to kicking, be able to control the ball at all times when it's in your possession. Stated another way, if you can't learn to control the ball, you can't learn to play soccer. In the opinion of the great Pele, ball control is the most important phase of the game. Considered to be soccer's greatest ball control artist, he claims that he's still learning more about it each game he plays.

Certainly ball control takes years to master. But as soon as you have learned how to kick accurately, you must learn the receiving or trapping of the ball. This action involves many aspects of simple ball control, particularly the method of gathering a loose ball "into close possession" (in range, close to your foot). In other words, trapping or receiving a pass involves techniques of deadening the bounce of the ball, reducing its speed, and/or bringing it down to the ground so that the ball can be kicked, passed, shot, or taken in your stride.

To progress in soccer skills, the techniques of bringing the ball under control quickly must be mastered. Accuracy in passing demands care. A player must always look for passing possibilities: if you can control the ball and cause it to drop dead at your feet, you'll have the time to look about and make accurate passes.

Another, and equally important, application of stopping techniques involves controlling the ball while moving or turning away from an opponent. If you attempt to trap a ball in front of an opponent, you're offering that opponent an opportunity to tackle and, at the same time, you're reducing the amount of time available for making an accurate pass. In soccer, space is time, and the more space a player makes for himself the greater amount of time he has to play and apply his techniques.

The basic principles of ball control are simple and few. They are:

1. Where possible you should be as close to the line of travel of the oncoming ball as possible. This means that footwork is important. If you fail to move into position and prefer to reach to control the ball, you're taking unnecessary risks.

2. You should decide, as soon as possible, how you intend to stop the ball. The greater your skill, the better equipped you are to change the play or method of attack or defense. The lower your skill level, the greater the need for an early choice.

3. That part of your body used to stop the ball should be as relaxed as possible. Before the ball strikes the stopping surface, that surface should be moving in the direction in which the ball is traveling. Failure to relax the stopping surface and move it before impact will cause the ball to bounce away out of control.

4. Your foot or body should be "angled" to direct the ball downwards. Once your body is in this position, the ball will be stilled or roll gently off in a chosen direction. However, remember to keep your eyes on the ball at all times.

If your intention is to control the ball and at the same time move off in a different direction, certain minor variations in technique are needed.

CONTROLLING THE BALL ON THE GROUND

The most important stop, certainly the most frequent, is of a ball that comes in on or just above the ground. This is where the passer is usually attempting to put it, unless he's setting you up for a head shot or pass. Most ground balls are stopped by either the sole of the foot or with the side of the foot.

With the Sole of the Foot   To stop a rolling ball with the sole of your foot, face the approaching ball and raise your foot slightly, bending the ankle of your stopping foot upward so that the sole of your foot is sloping forward at an angle. Angle your foot to allow the ball to fit into the space between your foot and the ground. The heel of your stopping foot should be about 2 or 3 inches off the ground. Your knee should be slightly bent and your entire body should be relaxed in a slight crouch. As the ball enters the "trap" between your sole and the turf, your foot is brought back slightly to cushion the impact. This movement tends to cause the ball to spin backwards slightly. Slight pressure

The simple sole-of-foot stop.

from your foot made as the ball is stopped will push the ball forward for you to move off immediately.

With the Side of the Foot To stop a rolling ball, as the ball approaches lift the stopping foot off the ground. When the ball strikes the foot lower it and move it backwards in one motion. After contact, the stopping foot continues to move backward, slowing the ball down until it can be stopped about 2 or 3 inches behind the point of original contact. The foot should be about 3 inches off the ground. If any lower, the ball may hop over the top of the foot, if any higher, it may slide underneath.

When controlling a ball on the ground with your foot, you'll frequently want to move off in directions other than straight ahead. Such moves are made in the same manner as in foot trap movements described later in this chapter.

CONTROLLING THE BALL IN THE AIR

The trapping technique is particularly useful when dealing with a ball dropping or falling down from the air. The parts of your body which are generally employed are the outside of the foot, the inside of the foot, the heel, thigh, chest, and head. The actual technique is approximately the same for all. The stopping or controlling surface must be

Cosmos player sprinting to meet the forward pass.

in line with the flight of the ball. As the ball approaches, the controlling surface must be relaxed and in motion to absorb the impact. One major fault in using the trapping technique is that a player will anticipate the arrival of the ball and move too soon, and the ball then bounces away, out of control.

The Inside-of-the-Foot Trap　To make successful foot traps, it is usually best to try to judge the flight of the ball and be "on the spot" when it strikes the ground. In making an inside-of-the-foot trap, your standing foot should be placed slightly to the rear of the point where you expect the ball to bounce. The trapping foot should be about 6 inches off the ground and the ball should be met at the moment it hits the ground. As the ball strikes your foot, the lower part of your leg and foot must be slightly angled over it, and sufficiently relaxed to smother any upward bounce. Don't jab the ball or you're almost certain to cause it to bounce away.

Frequently, when trapping a ball with the inside of the foot, you may want to move off in a sideways direction. For example, suppose you're trapping with your right foot and want to move off to the left. In such a case, place your standing (left) foot slightly to the rear and left of the point where the ball will fall to the ground. Begin to lean to the left as you raise your trapping (right) leg sideways and slightly forward. The instant the ball touches the ground, bring the trapping foot down on the outside of the ball and drag it with you while pivoting to the left. Any ball motion can be stopped by placing the side of your foot on the top of the ball.

You can also trap a ball with the inside of your foot as you move in the same direction the ball is traveling. This action is the same for moving off sideways except that your standing foot must be behind the ball, a little to the side for the trapping foot to drag the ball. Your body pivots on the standing foot and leans in the direction of the oncoming ball. As the ball strikes the ground, the leg of the trapping foot, raised and slightly bent, is brought lightly down on the outside of the ball. The pivot is completed and the trapping foot is swung smoothly alongside.

The Outside-of-the-Foot Trap   The ball can also be trapped with the outside-of-the-foot trap, which is executed in almost identical fashion as the inside-of-the-foot trap. Meet the ball as it strikes the ground, lean the foot and your lower leg over it to smother the bounce. If you wish to move off in a sideways direction, the same dragging principle is employed. If you're trapping with your right foot and plan to move to the right, place your standing (left) foot slightly behind and a little to the right of the ball. Your body should lean to the right and the trapping (right) leg is crossed in front of the standing one—again with your knee slightly bent and your foot horizontal. Your trapping foot is drawn in an easy swing across the front of the standing foot and continues in its stride. Your body should be in a slight crouch, but not tensed. If your foot doesn't make a clean trap, the outside of the leg may still force the ball to the ground.

In trapping a ball with the outside of the foot, the toe of your standing foot points where the ball will land, and this foot should be approximately 12 to 18 inches behind and to the side of the ball's landing spot. As the trapping foot controls the ball, your body pivots on the standing foot to permit your trapping foot to stride through.

Sole Trap   If the ball is falling too quickly for you to get into position to trap it with the inside of your foot, stretch your leg forward and trap the ball in front of you, using the sole of your foot. Place your standing foot slightly to the side and rear of where you anticipate the ball will bounce. Raise the trapping foot by bending your knee, but keep your toes pointing upwards. As the ball hits the ground, trap it

The making of
a chest trap.

by using a relaxed ankle joint and smother any bouncing action with the sole of your foot. If your knee is straightened slightly at contact, you'll feel a gentle push. This pushing action can be aided by a slight bending of the knee of your standing foot. As the ball is pushed forward, your balance is carried forward from your standing foot, and the trapping foot is brought to the ground for the first stride of your forward run.

If you can't quite get to the spot where the falling ball will drop, it's often possible to trap it as it bounces by pushing it down to the ground with your raised trapping foot.

If you're going to be challenged for the ball shortly after receiving it, it may be wise to trap the ball before it reaches the ground.

The Chest Trap   The lower part of your chest or stomach is used to bring a high-bouncing ball—or any ball about waist height—down to the ground quickly. From there, it can be controlled immediately by your foot. Move into the ball and take it just below your ribs. At the moment of contact, arch your body, drawing in your abdominal muscles by bending your shoulders forward. The impact of the ball is cushioned, and if this "folding" action is properly timed the ball will drop lightly to the ground. Any temptation to use your arms to form a pocket for the ball should be avoided because you run the risk of the ball hitting your arms, which is an infraction of one of the soccer rules.

When a high ball is dropping to the ground, you may not have time to step back to trap the ball with your foot. You can use the upper part of your chest to bring the ball under control. Place one foot in front of the other, which gives good balance. The ball is taken just below your chin, and the chest is allowed to sink downwards and backwards to cushion the ball so that it bounces only 3 or 4 inches before dropping to your feet. To lower the chest surface at impact, bend the knees slightly.

If you have to jump to reach the ball, make sure to jump slightly backwards and time the jump so that the ball strikes your chest when coming down. Again, withdraw your chest slightly on impact to reduce the speed of the ball. With practice, you'll be able to time your movement easily and, if required, deflect the ball in a sideways direction by turning your body at the proper moment.

Thigh Trap   While trapping a ball with the thigh was first looked upon by some coaches as a trick of showmanship, it has its uses, although they are somewhat limited. A badly bouncing ball can sometimes be pushed up in the air with the top part of your thigh so that your other leg can make a volley kick. By bouncing the ball more forcibly off your thigh, it can be lobbed over the head of your opponent.

A dropping ball coming at you at just below waist height is also a place to use a thigh trap. In this case, raise your leg, with the knee bent, and allow the ball to strike the softer part of your upper thigh. The desired cushioning effect is obtained by lowering the thigh slightly while relaxing the muscles at the precise moment of impact. The ball then rebounds only a couple of inches before dropping to the ground.

These various methods of trapping the ball to control it require delicacy and precision of touch. Close ball control, well performed, is the mark of a highly skilled player. But if you're not careful, a delay in trapping the ball can make your opponents' task very easy. Often the quick shot or pass will surprise the opposing team; or the stopping of the ball will give teammates time to cover you. The ability to sense when to control or when to play the ball quickly is one of the fine arts of the game.

Normally, you trap a ball for your own use. But a wayward ball can be brought under control for a teammate. For instance, you may be trapping the ball with the inside of your foot, when you realize that a teammate is well placed for a pass. The trapping action is given more sweep and the ball is sent along the ground to the other player. The trap with the inside of your foot may be used as a feint and the ball, at the last moment, can be pushed away with the outside of your foot in the opposite direction to a teammate. A ball which is being pulled down by the foot can be given a little more push and sent towards a teammate, or deflected towards another player. In the opinion of many sports writers, one of the most thrilling goals in the World Cup competition occurred in a match between England and Brazil in 1970. Late in the game, Brazil's Tostao had the ball to the left of the penalty area and Pele positioned himself in his favorite spot in front of goal. Millions of fans watching the game believed they knew the Brazilian strategy and so did the goalkeeper and the rest of the English team. The pass would go to Pele and he would attempt—and he had succeeded many times over the years—to get the ball into the net. The ball was flighted by Tostao to Pele, but instead of shooting for goal, as everyone expected, he made a perfect inside-the-foot trap and sent a short push pass to outside-right Jairzinho, who scored the winning goal.

Going to meet the ball is well demonstrated here.

(left) Prepared for a head ball with good balance and with the neck muscles set. *(right)* Power in a head ball involves proper contact, perfect timing, and a good follow-through.

HEADING

Although, at its best, soccer is played on the ground, the technique of heading is a most important skill. During a game, and particularly against a well organized defensive, it may be necessary to play the ball *over* the defenders rather than risk playing through narrow and well-guarded gaps on the ground. Some teams—and the New York Cosmos are one of them—rely heavily on scoring goals by following the heading techniques. The reason we do this is because of our striker, Randy Horton. He's 6 feet 2 inches tall, and due to his jumping skills, led the league in heading in 1972. This method is one of the most difficult for the goalkeeper to stop and is the most spectacular for the fans.

One question most asked by non-soccer players is, "Doesn't heading hurt?" The answer is "no"—if you do it properly. However, two basic rules must be followed:

1. *Keep your eyes on the ball at all times.*   Your natural reflex action is to close your eyes as the ball comes toward you. Constant practice will teach you to keep them open until contact. The correct part of your head to use is the forehead. The flatness of the forehead enables you to be accurate in directing the ball.

2. *Never let the ball hit you—you must hit the ball.*   This means that as the ball comes toward you, you must tense your neck muscles and

hit at the ball with your forehead, and not just stand still and let the ball hit you. The forward nodding of your head, when combined with a forward movement of the body, is a very powerful movement.

When learning to head the ball it's better to use a soft soccer ball or, better still, a plastic ball, until you begin to gain confidence. A good, simple practice to start with is to throw a ball 2 feet above the head and, as it falls, head it back into the air, trying each time to head it higher. More height can be obtained by pushing your head and neck forward to meet the ball. Bracing your neck muscles gives more power. But remember that this is only practice to help in gaining confidence. In a real game, no player has to head the ball straight into the air.

Once you have confidence, it's important to learn to jump for a ball and head it in any direction. If you stand still, with both feet on the ground, and wait for the ball, you'll have beaten yourself. Against a good opponent, you'll never touch the ball because your opponent will simply jump and head the ball away. It is a common fault to watch your opponent, who is also trying to head the ball, instead of watching the ball. The first basic rule of heading is: never take your eyes off the ball.

To be good "in the air," the timing of your jump is vital and needs a great deal of practice. Use a short run and jump up from one foot. This gives greater height than a standard jump using both feet. In achieving maximum height in a jump, the basic techniques which apply to the high jump procedure in track apply here, too. In other words, the stride onto your take-off foot is a long one, with your body leaning back. The weight shifts as you rock back to your take-off foot from heel to toe. As your take-off leg extends, powerfully, your other knee is swung forward and upwards—equally powerfully. A forward, upward swing of both arms will assist momentum. In some cases, of course, you must jump almost vertically, and lean slightly backwards in your last stride so that your body will be coming into a vertical position as your standing leg straightens. The take-off is made by placing your heel in the ground and then rocking forward onto the ball of your foot.

In all jumps, the body, head, and neck should be in cocked or coiled position to hit the ball. To do this, it's usually a good idea to kick both legs backward and upward just after take-off. This causes your entire spine to arch backward. From this position, in which you appear to hang in air, your upper body is jack-knifed forward at the hips and the normal snapping forward of your head occurs.

There are occasions, of course, when you don't have time to prepare running jumps. At such times, a stand jump must be used. But the

The player who "climbs" the highest generally wins the ball.

problem here is in overcoming inertia, and whenever possible you should be moving, however slightly, if you're likely to receive the ball. This applies to all circumstances in which the ball may come to you, but particularly when you're likely to have to jump off both your feet. Incidentally, when heading without any challenge, you frequently use the momentum of your jump to add power to your heading action. You must control the natural tendency to raise the arms forward as the take-off is made, to avoid pushing any opponents.

The follow-through position for off-the-ground head-balling after contact has been made.

In Chapter 9, there are several heading exercises that you should practice. Once you've mastered the basic techniques of heading you'll be able to employ it under the following game conditions:

Heading Forward When the ball is dropping and you're standing nearly underneath it, your head must turn upward to follow it. As a result the ball, as your head hits it, has the tendency to rebound upward. To prevent this, you must sway back, bending your body and extending your head. You can follow the ball carefully, and then swing

Two fine action shots of clearance headers.

forward with a powerful motion of the upper portion of your body. Your head will come forward, following through with a strong punch; your neck muscles will be braced to take the impact. Make sure that your eyes continue to follow the flight of the ball. The arms, which are held forward as your body sways back, should be pulled back with your elbows bent to help in the striking action of your head. As in all striking actions, you should head through the ball and continue the follow-through in the direction of intended line of flight.

To change the direction of the ball your neck and head are turned so that contact is still made with the same part of your forehead. The decision to head the ball must be made early, whenever possible, in order that your neck and head can be positioned for a powerful and controlled striking motion.

Heading Downwards   To head the ball downwards, your head must start from well behind the ball. The ball is allowed to fall in front of your body so that the flat of your forehead is directed downwards at the moment your head hits the ball. This action is difficult to time accurately. If the strike is made too early, the ball will glance off the top of your head. If the hit is a moment too late, the ball may hit your nose. When jumping to meet the ball, it's even more difficult to get strength to the movement, for it must all come from the swing of your body and a very short nod of your head.

The Diving Header   You shouldn't attempt to head a low ball if a nearby player is likely to attempt to kick it. It would be physically dangerous to yourself, and you might be penalized for dangerous play, particularly as the other player is almost obliged to hold back his kick for safety. But you may find that the only way of seizing a scoring chance is to fling yourself in a dive to head a ball which you can't possibly reach with your toe. Or you may be forced to head a low ball to protect your goal, or as a last effort to intercept the ball.

Back-Heading   This technique is often employed by a forward to make a surprise attempt on goal when he is standing with his back towards it. Similarly, when heading forward might allow an opposing player a shot at the goal from close range, a defender dealing with a high ball may decide to head backwards to a teammate or to the goalkeeper.

To accomplish the back-heading technique, the ball is played with the upper part of your forehead where the forehead begins to slope back onto the top of your head. This permits the ball to be played firmly,

(top) Eyes are on the
ball going for a low
or diving header. *(center)*
Eyes are still on the ball as the
player makes good contact
with his forehead. *(bottom)*
It is very important to cushion
the fall by using the hands.

Speed is important in soccer. Here Willie Mfum, one of the Cosmos' fastest men, streaks past opposition players en route for the goal.

and also the ball may be followed for as long as possible. Where contact is made further back on your head you can't see what you're doing. The motion of your head, neck, and trunk are exactly the opposite of those employed in the forward heading movement. Obviously, the degree of control in this technique is limited and its only real advantage is in surprise.

Heading to Deflect the Ball　　This is often used when a ball is played at a fairly rapid speed. In such cases, you may wish to deflect the ball without reducing the speed to any degree. Your intentions are to deflect the ball slightly away from a defender so that an attacking teammate can run on and collect the ball in his stride.

To achieve deflection heading, the ball is played with the side of your forehead where it forms a corner with the side of your head. Your head itself hardly moves at all and the ball is allowed to glance off it. Some players, such as our Willie Mfum and Everald Cummings, have developed a flicking technique with the sides of their heads which is a combination of power and deflection heading. This produces a result which is difficult to anticipate and is often effective in taking a headed shot at goal from a fast cross. Opposing players are not sure whether the forward is going to play the ball with the full face of his forehead or whether he is going to deflect or, as is often the case, use a combination of the two.

Cosmos' Jorge Siega protects the ball by keeping his body between the ball and the opponent.

RUNNING WITH THE BALL AND DRIBBLING

A distinction—however arbitrary it may seem—should be made between running with the ball and dribbling. Clearly, there is all the difference in the world between controlling the ball when running fast, turning and reversing without immediate challenge, and the action of beating another player while in possession of the ball. To dribble, both speed and ball control must be augmented with the ability to elude or deceive opponents.

RUNNING WITH THE BALL

Every player on a team, with the possible exception of the goalkeeper, should be able to run fairly fast with the ball in close control at his feet so that he can stop and move about with ease. Fast running speed can be attained by playing the ball with the outside of the controlling foot each time it comes forward in its stride. You must be able to do this type of running while sizing up the situation around you, and must therefore develop a feel for the control of the ball rather than looking at it all the time.

(top) On the dribble, it is wise sometimes to approach an opponent at right angles with the ball under control. (bottom) Then cut inside, playing the ball with the left side of the instep. Note that the opponent is "caught" on the wrong foot.

How to dribble past an opponent by pushing the ball through his legs.

A track sprinter, of course, gathers speed in a few short steps, after which the length of his stride scarcely varies. But as a soccer player you'll seldom have the opportunity to settle in a straight course. Your running will consist primarily of a series of short bursts. The length of your strides will vary, and the planting of your foot for stopping, moving around, and kicking will often bring you off your toes onto your heels or the soles of your feet. When checking a run you should be able to turn the ball obliquely backward to avoid the tackling foot of your opponent. In the same way you should be able to use the sole of your foot to stop the ball quickly, so that you're ready to play it again immediately. You may want to tap the ball forward to break into another sprint or even to pull the ball further back to enable you to turn and run in the opposite direction.

The best form of "running" exercise, such as described in Chapter 9, should be closely related to those of actual game conditions. A quick reaction in accelerating from a slow to a fast pace may give you an advantage over a defender who is chasing you. You should develop the ability to slow down as you approach a defender and then, with a push from the outside of your foot, send the ball past him and break into a sprint.

DRIBBLING

Dribbling, as in basketball, is the technique of getting past one or more opponents by keeping the ball under complete control while making

When approaching an opponent who is standing square *(top left)* a quick, controlled inside-of-the-foot pass *(top right)* on the outside of the opponent. Then follow with a short burst to go inside and past the opponent (bottom) to meet up with the ball.

Cosmos' Josef Jelinek prepares to pull the ball away from the defender with the sole of his shoe.

deceptive changes in direction and speed. The different ways in which this can be attempted are limitless, but the basic principles which must be kept in mind are:

1. You must be able to keep the ball within comfortable playing distance. This distance will be determined by the ease with which you can move the ball in any direction through a full circle and remain within playing distance of it.

2. You should be in an evenly balanced position in order to move in any direction. This particularly applies when you're waiting for your opponent to make the first move. Close observation of any good dribbler will show him making continuous attempts to throw his opponent off balance. Some, like the Cosmos' Jorge Siega, do this by tapping the ball from one foot to another. They are tempting the defender into a tackle or causing him to continually transfer his weight from one foot to the other. Others employ twisting movements of the hips and shoulders to give an opponent the impression that they are about to pass rather than dribble past him.

3. At all times you should try to make your opponent move into an off-balance position. This is the equivalent to deke, or fake, in that

you pretend to move in one direction when you really intend to move in another. You do this by various movements of your feet and body aimed at causing your opponent to react and block your direction of travel.

A change of pace is one of the simplest ways of making a fake. As the defender draws close, you accelerate your running. This actual change of pace may be sufficient to elude an opponent who is slow in reacting, but if you can induce your opposing defender to make a tackle, you can move away the instant he is off balance. Keep in mind that a good defender will have quick powers of recovery; therefore, you must learn to time your fake exactly and make it look like the real thing. Your own reaction must be instantaneous: your get-away must start as soon as the defender responds. The sure defender won't tackle unless he feels he has a good chance of retrieving the ball; you must appear to offer him that chance and put the speed of your reaction against his. You may use a teammate as a further decoy, faking to pass to him and then dashing away in another direction.

The process of beating a man is so complicated that you can't give conscious thought to its separate factors. You must practice methods of faking till they have become automatic, and you'll have experienced defenders' responses till you know instinctively when you have succeeded in getting an opponent to make a false move.

Two other popular dribbling techniques are screening and showing the ball. The latter involves your deliberately encouraging your opponent to challenge or tackle for the ball by making him think that you can't control it effectively. This often can be achieved by pushing the ball towards your opponent and perhaps drawing it away. An important part of this is controlling the ball with the sole of your foot. This enables a fake to be made at the ball while letting it *apparently* roll out of reach.

When screening the ball, your body is placed between your opponent and the ball while keeping it within playing reach. For example, you may have attempted to dribble past an opponent face to face and failed. The next time you might use a screening technique in order to make tackling by your opponent rather more difficult. Alternatively, you might screen your opponent from the ball while holding it and waiting for teammates to move into supporting positions for a pass.

One of the methods which an experienced defender will use against a good dribbler is to retreat towards his own goal, particularly when he knows his opponent to be quick and clever. He does this in order to be already moving in the direction in which he knows his opponent will move, and also to join up with the other defenders. The intelligent defender will also try to jockey his opponent into a small space where his opponent is restricted by the sideline, the goal line, or both. A good retreating defender will usually cause you to slow down, and you should be aware of this. The ability to dribble fast towards a retreating opponent and then to beat him, perhaps by increasing speed, requires a great deal of practice. Too often dribblers permit defenders to dictate to them: when you have the ball be aware of this, and prevent the defender from dominating the situation. For a defender faced by a player in possession of the ball there is a considerable problem presented when the attacker moves toward him rather than, as is more often the case, away. The defender can't allow you to move towards him indefinitely: sooner or later he must do something—which is what the player with the ball should be waiting for. Changing direction at speed, as previously mentioned, is a difficult but important dribbling technique.

In running past an opponent with the ball many different techniques can be used. Some defenders, in concentrating on anticipating an opponent's dribbling movement, stand with their legs wide open. It may be possible to play the ball through the defender's legs while running past him. Pele, when dribbling, often gives the appearance of trying to play the ball against an opponent's legs before moving on to collect the rebound. Similarly, it's possible to push the ball past an opponent while running around and past him on the opposite side. This ability to move very quickly over 10 or 15 yards, frequently from a standing position, is very important in developing dribbling skill.

In summary, to be a good dribbler you must possess speed and quick reactions in running with the ball, speed and delicacy of touch in ball control, and the ability to dodge, swerve, and turn at will. You must have a sense of guile based on a knowledge of opponents' reactions to various movements, the ability to work in a confined space, and the confidence to face up to rigorous tackling.

THE THROW-IN

The throw-in is more than just a means of putting the ball back into play after it has gone out. As described in Chapter 7, the throw-in has an important attacking value. True, a score can't be obtained by throw-

(top left) Preparing for a throw-in.
Hold the ball with both hands
firmly placed as illustrated. (top right)
The proper position for a throw-in: ball held
behind head and feet placed behind the line.
(bottom) Completion of the throw-in.
The ball has to be released immediately
as it passes over the center of the head;
then the arms follow through.

ing the ball into the goal, but a long throw can place the ball directly into your opponents' goal area to set up chances for your teammates to score. The rules of soccer state that "the thrower shall deliver the ball from over his head." You should make sure that there's no doubt about this by taking the ball well behind your head before throwing it, even though the ball doesn't leave the hands until they're in front of your body. Keep in mind that if you make the throw incorrectly—a foul throw—you're not given a second attempt. The ball goes over to the opposing team to be thrown in.

To make the throw, hold the ball in your hands with the fingers comfortably outspread, so that their thrust—when the final throw is made—will be behind the ball. Most players prefer to stand with the feet slightly apart. Your knees should be bent forward to counterbalance your body as it bends backwards. The arms should be bent behind your head and the heels of your feet should be slightly off the ground. A rapid straightening of your legs should coincide with a strong forward movement of your upper body. The motion culminates in a powerful swing of your arms and a final snap of your hands and fingers as you throw the ball forward.

Remember that both your hands should be used in throwing the ball. It is wrong to throw in the ball with one hand even though the other is touching or guiding the ball.

You may raise your heels or drag your foot in making a throw, but you must have part of each foot on the ground, on or outside the sideline, at the time the throw-in is made. Players who have one or both feet on the line when throwing may, by raising their heels, have the part of the foot touching the ground in the field of play and not on the line, which is against the rules. It is to your own advantage to take a stance for throwing well outside the sideline, particularly when by picking up the ball and throwing it quickly you can start an immediate attack on the opposing goal. Unless the ball passes across the sideline into the field of play directly from the throw-in, it must be thrown again because it hasn't been thrown in, according to rules.

TACKLING

This may seem more like a football term than a soccer term, but tackling in soccer isn't the same as in football. Soccer tackling is one of the three ways of getting possession of the ball when on defense.

The first way is by interception. This is done by cutting off a pass

(top left) This stance is allowed because the rule states that part of both feet should be on the ground when the throw is being made. *(top right)* This isn't allowed because the feet must be on or behind the line when the throw is being taken. *(bottom left)* The throw-in rule also states that the feet must face into the field of play, thus this position is legal. *(bottom right)* This is an illegal position because the feet run parallel to the line and don't face it.

An illegal charge on a Dallas defender by Barry Mahy, the Cosmos' Captain.

before it reaches another opponent. To be successful, the interceptor must be alert and able to move quickly to the ball. The sense of when to go forward to the ball and when to wait will grow out of playing experience. If failing to intercept a ball you go for, you, as a defender, will have given your man a "free pass" to get by you.

The second method is the shoulder charge, a contact between your shoulder and your opponent's shoulder. If your arm isn't close against your side, then you're nudging your opponent, and this is a foul. If you charge your opponent in his back, that is also a foul. The contact must be shoulder to shoulder. Sometimes only a slight brush is necessary to tip a player off his balance; but the experienced player usually senses when a charge is about to be made and braces himself for it by leaning towards the tackler, meeting charge with charge. You should use the outside leg to give a strong push-off, and if you miss contact you can use your other leg to prevent yourself from falling. Your opponent should be charged when his weight is on the outside leg so that he can't recover quickly.

The third method is, of course, tackling, which is done only with the feet. You can go in as hard and as fast as you like, but you must kick at the ball and not at the opponent. However, players will often come into hard contact with each other at the moment they're both kicking at the ball.

When considering tackling, you should try to maneuver your opponent into a position where:

1. The least possible danger will arise if the tackle fails.

2. The space in which the player with the ball can dodge, turn, or avoid the tackle is as small as possible.

3. Other defending teammates are available to cover you.

4. You can decide when the timing advantage is on your side. Usually the best time to tackle is at the moment when your opponent is attempting to control the ball, before he can do what he likes with it, and before he starts running with it. If he has full control and you rush at him, he has only to turn the ball to one side. You are beaten and he runs past you.

All players have certain strengths and weaknesses, and these should be carefully studied. For instance, most players prefer to use one foot when controlling the ball. Even good two-footed players show this preference and the more difficult the situation the more they'll use the foot in which they have the greatest confidence. If you can jockey your opponent in the direction of his weaker foot, you'll be in the best position to tackle effectively, for while his controlling movements are being made with his "good" foot you can force him in a direction in which, sooner or later, he may be compelled to use his "bad" foot. Close observation of players will also reveal their inclination towards certain types of faking motions. These are usually developed, almost as habits, to enable a player to move in the direction in which he wants to go. Great players, of course, can move in any direction with equal facility, but even these have a liking for a certain direction and a certain foot.

Actually, dribbling and tackling have something in common. Both skills are learned mainly from game experience. You can become familiar with the physical impacts and learn the basic technique of both dribbling and tackling by synthetic practice, but the real test of skill lies in your ability to get past an opponent or to dispossess an opponent who is equally determined to give a tackle or evade the tackle—a circumstance rarely met outside a game.

Different tackling techniques tend to be more common in different phases of the game. Here are some of the more popular ways of tackling.

FRONT BLOCK TACKLE

When your opponent is approaching, you make your tackle either to beat him to the ball or to block the ball at the moment he's playing it. If you try to block the ball, you must get your body weight well over it so that the tackling foot can be used forcefully. If possible, lean your body over the ball to bring your shoulder into contact with your opponent. The inside of your foot plays the ball with your knee turned outwards: this provides the largest possible blocking surface. Both knees are slightly bent to absorb the shock of the tackling impact and also to lower your center of gravity, which places you in a position in which you'll be difficult to overbalance—if, for instance, a shoulder charge is attempted at the same time as your tackle. If you tackle with your leg outstretched, you'll either lean away from the tackle or throw the body weight partly on to your tackling foot. In the former case, the resistance power is reduced; in the latter, your leg is put in a vulnerable position for strains and other injuries.

When the ball is wedged between your foot and that of your opponent, be sure to maintain a firm pressure against the ball while leaning into it. At this point one of you will try to obtain possession of the ball in one or more of the following ways:

1. By dragging the ball out of the tackle sideways.
2. By forcing the ball between the opponent's feet.
3. By rolling or lifting the ball over the opponent's foot.
4. By shoulder charging in such a manner so as to cause the opponent to lose balance. Strong tacklers will frequently wait for their opponent to try to change the application of force against the ball and use this momentary release of force to gain possession themselves.

One of the most common faults in front block tackling is deciding to lunge at the ball when the opponent is well balanced and slightly out of reach. This places your opponent at an advantage, since you can't apply controlled force against the ball. Depending on your distance away from the ball, your tackling leg is straight and your weight is entirely committed to one foot: you can't adjust your position and you

Cosmos' Roby Young makes an inside-of-the-foot tackle.

can't recover should your opponent resist or evade the tackle successfully.

THE SIDE BLOCK TACKLE

This tackle is usually required when your opponent is running away with the ball and you are approaching him from behind. The principles of the front block tackle are employed, but you must try to ensure that you're as close as possible to the ball before you commit yourself. If possible, your non-tackling foot should be level with or slightly in front of the ball as you pivot on it to bring yourself into the block tackling position, and your body should pivot quickly and powerfully on your standing foot in order to develop enough momentum to overcome or resist the running momentum of your opponent.

By overtaking your man, you can still make a block tackle by pivoting as your tackling leg swings into the ball. You veer slightly outward until, in your last stride, you bring your standing foot in a little ahead of the ball. Pivot on this foot as your tackling leg plays the ball. You may find it easier to use the instep rather than the side of your foot in playing the ball. You must still keep your body crouched, otherwise your momentum will cause you to fall backwards at the slightest contact with your opponent.

A sliding tackle being executed and a shot was on goal immediately.

When running behind your opponent, the back-heel tackle may be used under certain conditions. The heel tackle is made using the foot nearest to your opponent, but can only be made when your opponent is controlling the ball with the foot which is nearest to you. As the two of you are running along side by side, you move your tackling leg over the ball and block it with your heel as it touches the ground.

You can also tackle with the outside of the foot: in the same position as for the heel tackle, your inside foot is used and the ball is blocked by turning your foot outward as your opponent attempts to play the ball.

SLIDING TACKLE

As a player with the ball runs away from an opponent who he knows is trying to get into a tackling position, he will often transfer the ball to the foot which is furthest away from the tackler. This makes the block tackle extremely difficult, if not impossible, to execute. In these circumstances you may have to use a sliding tackle; but keep in mind that the sliding tackle is usually employed as a desperate measure to combat dangerous developments in attacking play. It's most frequently seen when an attacker has broken clear of the defense and is running towards goal with the ball. In these circumstances you may feel that if you take the time necessary to get into a block tackling position your opponent may have been given enough time to take a shot at the goal. In this situation you must prevent the shot by sliding the ball away to another defender or, more usually, out of play. Since when using a sliding tackle you'll be on the ground and, therefore, should the tackle fail, out of the play momentarily, you must be certain of success, or alternatively, the situation must be so dangerous that any attempt, however great the risk, must be made. Here are the basics of this method of tackling:

1. You must be as near to your opponent as circumstances permit.
2. Your tackling leg is the one furthest away from your opponent, and you go to ground with your weight supported by the leg and thigh which you'll employ as your tackling leg.
3. The tackle is usually made after your opponent has played the ball forward or before he attempts to play it.
4. You usually veer slightly away from your opponent before committing yourself to the slide across the ball's line of travel.

Since your tackling leg is in contact with the ground while it is stretched into the tackle there is little chance of injury. The purpose of this tackle is to slide the ball away from an opponent; but there is also the possibility of sliding into a form of block tackle. In this technique the following considerations must be kept in mind:

1. You must be close to the man with the ball.
2. You should prepare to go into the tackle with your inside leg doubled up. As the tackle begins, you take your weight upon that leg and, often, the hand on that side of your body. Your tackling (outside) leg is swung across as you lean in towards your opponent and the inside of your foot is used to block the ball. Stability is maintained because you're in the lowest possible position on the ground. By the same token, should you make a slight error in judgment, you're fully committed and out of the play.

Sliding tackles are rather desperate methods of challenging for the ball and entail risks. The main risk involves an error of judgment,

(top) Dangerous play on white for bending too low; (bottom) while dangerous play on black for high kicking.

whereby the ball is missed and a defender is momentarily out of action. The second involves the possibility of tripping an opponent which, in certain circumstances, can bring about exactly that which the tackle is designed to prevent, a goal being scored from a free kick or a penalty kick. But if a sliding tackle is executed properly, there is no danger either to your opponent or to you. The tackle shouldn't be confused with the double jump at the ball, which has obvious dangers, particularly when the feet are thrust at the legs of the opponent. This move, even if no contact is made with the other player, may be penalized.

Tackling and struggling for possession of the ball is a vital and exciting part of soccer. Some players, such as the Cosmos' Werner Roth, Rochester's Peter Short, Dallas' John Best, and St. Louis' John Sewell, are well prepared by temperament to become strong tacklers. These are the aggressive players who are confident in their physical attributes. They're not necessarily all big men but they are all full of determination.

5

Techniques of
Goalkeeping

THE goalkeeper has an extremely difficult and responsible position to play. If this is your position, you need courage and the ability to make quick decisions. A ball can be shot at a goal with tremendous speed (up to 80 m.p.h.), giving you little time to react to make a save. Frequently your view of the ball will be obstructed until the last split second, or the ball may be deflected on its path to the goal so that you must change the direction of your movement rapidly. While your judgment of a situation and your sense of anticipation can help greatly, the speed of your reaction and agility in flinging yourself at the ball are very important factors. You should never give up and think that you're beaten. You must train your instincts to make every effort to stop the "unstoppable" shot or to prevent a score in a "hopeless" attacking situation. Do this and you'll be surprised how much success you'll have in your goaltending activities. Remember this when you are practicing and attempt to make every save as though you were playing in the NASL Championship Final, for it is by this type of practice that you will acquire the nerve and split-second timing required for top-notch performance in goal.

Over the years there has been a great deal of controversy by soccer experts over the height of goalkeepers. We would like to point out that perhaps two of the best goaltenders since World War II have been 5-foot-5-inch Da Rui, the French international player, and 6-foot-4-inch Yashin of the Moscow Dynamo. The two goalkeepers on our 1972 Championship team were 5-foot-6-inch Emanuel Kofie and 6-foot Richard Blackmore. In our opinion, height is not as important as agility and a safe pair of hands. True, a tall, agile goalie with a good pair

Cosmos' goalkeeper, Richie Blackmore, in a typical goalie anticipatory position.

of hands has certain distinct advantages—for example the extent of his reach in fielding the high ball and in stretching to make saves in goal.

CATCHING OR FIELDING THE BALL

The Golden Rule of goaltending is: safety first. Two hands should always be used rather than one. And, whenever possible, get your body behind the hands to create a second barrier to the ball. It is best to attempt to catch and hold the ball if you can. Never develop the habit of hitting the ball with the palms of your hands to bounce it on the ground or to push it sideways. Even when diving sideways to save a shot you should always try to hold the ball. A ball that bounces from a goalkeeper's hands or body is likely to be kicked into goal by a nearby attacking player.

A goalie is, of course, required to catch or field the ball at all heights and angles from ground level to a height which requires a full upward or sideways leap.

Fielding a Low Ball   Whenever possible, you should position yourself directly in front of the oncoming ball. The legs should be kept close together and the hands placed—palms upward—under the ball. Some goalkeepers prefer to bend their legs slightly while others like to keep the legs almost straight. For the beginning goalkeeper we usually recommend the former since you can usually move more quickly after fielding the ball when the legs are slightly bent. In either case, as soon as the hands grasp the ball they are brought up towards the chest so that the ball is securely held. This is especially important when there is the possibility of an immediate challenge from an attacking player.

In some cases, such as a hard low shot and ground balls, it is a good idea to turn both your feet sideways to the direction of the shot and bend down on one knee. Your upper body should be twisted full face towards the path of the oncoming ball and your hands, palms upwards, should be at ground level, backed up by your legs, waiting to guide the ball into your chest or stomach. This bending position, with no gaps between your knees through which the ball could squeeze if you mishandle it, presents the biggest possible stopping surface to the ball and your eyes will be close to the ball's line of flight. This position also permits you to grab the ball and move away fairly quickly. Any kneeling position in which the knees are towards the ball should be avoided since it may result in the ball bouncing away from your control. Always get onto your feet as quickly as possible so that you're prepared to avoid or withstand a collision with an opponent without going over the line into your goal. Remember that the position of your feet isn't important, but if you carry the ball over the goal line, it's a score for your opponents.

Catching a Waist-High Ball   If you have time, position yourself to catch a waist-high shot with your body backing your hands. The hands, as with low shots, are held palms upward so that the ball can be hugged to the chest or pulled into the stomach.

Catching a Chest-High Ball   The same catching technique is required as with a waist-high ball. Lean slightly forward so that the force of the shot won't push you backward, off balance, as you clasp the ball tightly to your chest. Some goalies have problems when the ball tends to bounce away from them on chest-high shots. To prevent this, they place one hand above and one below the ball. The ball can be caught similarly under the chin and the goalie may often jump up to take fairly high balls in this fashion. The same technique is often employed by goaltenders when diving sideways to a ball close enough to be protected by the body. The same grip, bringing the ball to your body, can also be used when falling sideways onto the ball.

Catching an Overhead Ball   Always try to face the flight of the ball,

The proper method of gathering a ground ball. It's most important to make sure not to leave any gaps through which the ball could squeeze if it were mishandled. In the illustration, below, note how the goalkeeper's arms and legs are set to avoid or withstand a collision.

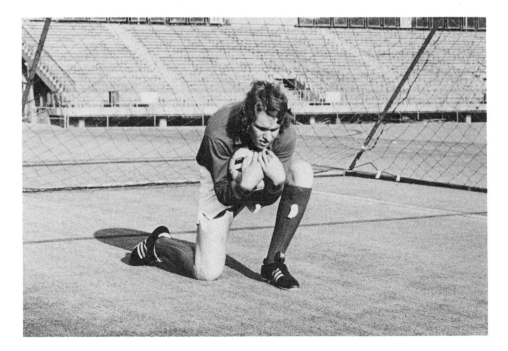

your hands raised in the direction of it, the palms pointing toward it. That is, you reach up with both hands behind the ball, the fingers outspread. If the shot is hard, allow your hands to recede slightly to absorb the force of it, and catch it slightly in front of the body. The path of the ball must be judged carefully and watched right into the hands, particularly when you have to jump. As soon as your hands take the ball, it should be brought down to a clutching position on your chest.

One of the most difficult goaltending skills to master is that of leaping to catch a ball above the heads of the attackers. You must judge the flight of the ball precisely, leap with power, and grasp the ball securely in your hands at the full height of your leap. Tipping the ball over the bar or around the upright and pushing the ball away are occasionally necessary. They may look more spectacular, but the goalie most respected by attacking players is one who is an expert catcher.

When planning to catch a high ball, go after it as soon as possible: don't stand around waiting for the ball to come to you. This gives you the advantage of getting to it early, and a forward movement will allow you to jump higher and more effectively off your best jumping foot. Whenever there is the likelihood of having to go for the ball you should be moving on your feet in some way, however slightly; in doing so you have overcome the inertia of your body weight and the resultant run, spring, or jump will be quicker and higher.

Diving Catches The most spectacular of all of the goalkeeper's catches are the diving saves. They are accomplished in much the same manner as catching a high ball, except that your movement is along a horizontal plane rather than a vertical one. When you are diving for the ball, kick your legs upward to make certain that when landing a part of the upper body—hands, arms, or shoulders—touches the ground first. It's a good idea to get the ball to the ground as quickly as possible after catching it by moving your arms downward so that the forearm and the ball are first to hit the ground, while the upper hand pushes the ball down. As soon as possible, pull the ball in to your chest to prevent its rolling loose.

When facing a diving save situation, as with all other saves, if you're not completely sure of your ability to hold onto the ball, deflect or punch it away from the goal. While there are many spectacular dives and flying leaps you'll do in making saves, in these basic moves your goalkeeping motto should be "Sure and safe; not flashy."

Making a save on
a waist-high shot *(left)*
and chest-high shot *(right)*.

DEFLECTING A BALL OVER THE BAR OR AROUND THE POST

As stated before, there are times when it is too risky for a goalkeeper to catch a high ball close to goal. Such balls are best deflected over the crossbar or around the post. While two-handed deflection is safer, there is a little extra stretch to be gained by using only one hand over the head. In both cases the palm is used. Flicking the ball with the hand and punching the ball over the bar are not recommended. There is always the danger that the ball may skid off the knuckles into the goal. To do it properly, you leap as though to catch the ball, but as it makes contact with the palm and fingers, the hand is turned to guide it over the bar, using a slightly upward pushing motion. But make sure that the ball goes over the crossbar: in a recent international game, a well-known goalkeeper carelessly pushed the ball onto the face of the bar so that it bounced back into play and resulted in the only score of the game.

When facing a hard shot that is going just under the bar, you may have to deflect it over the bar for safety. The best method, if you have time, is to jump with one hand "following" the ball and guiding it over the crossbar as you turn your body toward the ball to keep it completely in sight. Often, though, a hard shot will not give you time to think:

When catching a high ball, always try to face the direction of the shot and place the hands slightly to the back of the ball. Note how the goalkeeper raises one knee slightly as a protective measure to keep away opponents who may run into him. After catching the ball, he'll bring it down and clasp it to his chest in one movement.

you will simply try to make a reaction save, just getting any part of your outstretched hand to the ball.

PUNCHING A BALL

When several players jump together to head the ball the goalie is bound to have great difficulty in reaching it to catch it; and in the general bustle he may drop it. It is best to leap and make a vigorous punch at the ball. But when punching the ball you should, whenever possible, use both fists together. This makes for a bigger and flatter punching surface and the contact which results is safer and more accurate. Occasionally, however, and particularly when dealing with high crosses, you have to punch the ball away with only one hand. Always attempt not to punch across the flight of the ball—either hit it back in the direction from which it came or, if it's going across the face of the goal, aid it on its merry way.

SMOTHERING THE BALL

Whenever you fall to the ground to hold a ball with your hands, your first action should be to pull the ball quickly in to your body for safe protection. In smothering the ball at a forward's feet, you should again try to get your body near to your hands as they grab at the ball. Get

to your feet, keeping the ball tightly hugged to the body, and then dodge out of the way of the opposing player to make your clearance.

When an attacking forward approaches the goal, you never dive straight forward at his feet, for two very good reasons. First, you need to protect your head and, second, you need to go down with your body behind the ball in a sideways position so as to cover a wider area of the goal. In other words, try to produce the largest and longest wall possible behind the ball. But, if the attacker has let the ball run too far in front of him, you should fall over the ball, grabbing it to you, to place your body between the ball and the opponent, with the ball clutched firmly and your back to the attacker.

CLEARING A BALL

Once in possession of the ball, the goalkeeper is allowed to hold it for a maximum of four steps before he must kick it or throw it clear. This is an international and pro rule. Colleges, high schools, and other youth leagues sometimes have less strict rules, although the trend is toward complete standardization within North America to pro rules.

In making a diving save, be sure to pull the ball into the chest to prevent its rolling loose at the feet of opponents who may be waiting nearby for just such a slip.

When tipping the ball over
the crossbar, use the palm of
the hand or the fingertips and
give the ball a slightly upward
pushing motion.

Remember that once the goalkeeper has the ball his team is on the offensive, and to lose possession for the sake of getting distance is a bad tactic.

Too frequently, goalkeepers kick the ball high in the air and far upfield on the theory: the farther the safer. If you give possession to your opposition, you will find that you're back where you started, saving another shot. Certainly the goalkeeper will sometimes want to kick for distance—for instance when his team has a tall, tough forward like the Cosmos' Randy Horton. But if you want to keep possession, it is best to throw the ball out.

Greater accuracy can be achieved for throws over 25 yards by throwing over-arm to the receiver's feet. For throws of longer distances, you can use the javelin-type throw (see illustration) or the under-arm roll, as in bowling, for shorter distances. But the longer the throw, the longer the time that you need to prepare yourself for it and the longer the time for your opponents to move and anticipate it. Short, accurate, hard, low throws are better than long, inaccurate, soft, high throws. Don't attempt a lob pass except when you must throw it over the head of an opponent to reach a teammate.

PROPER POSITIONING

All of our best goalkeepers seem to know the art of proper positioning. Most shots appear to come straight at them and they have to do

The goalkeeper's one-fist punch *(left)* and two-fist punch *(right)*.

very little leaping or diving after the ball. In other words, they make most saves look easy. To accomplish this, you must understand the duties of all your defenders and must be equally capable of reading the plays of the opposing attacking team. A highly developed sense of anticipation both in positioning and in moving is essential to a goalkeeper. You must always be ready for the unexpected to happen, for a sliced kick, or a deflection. Such occasions test your quickness of reaction and your agility. Of course none of this helps too much when you come across forwards able to make the ball "bend" in flight. Pele and the great Portuguese Eusebio are outstanding and adept at this skill. Our own Siggy Stritzl is also famous for this same skill. Siggy, in fact, scored the first Cosmos' home goal by curving a "banana shot" around the Washington Darts' wall in 1971 as the Darts' goalkeeper threw himself out of proper position.

Normally, the goalie reacts only when he sees the ball approaching. But goalkeeping is much more than the quick reflex save. A goalkeeper who stays on his goal line all the time is giving away his great advantage of being able to handle the ball with his hands within the entire penalty area. He should, in fact, leave the goal whenever he sees the chance of getting the ball. He should also come off his goal line when a forward is approaching him with the ball.

When an opposing attacking player is in a shooting position, your major task is to present him with the smallest possible target. In a

The goalie using the lofted kick to clear the ball.

frontal position, where you're standing in the center of your net on the goal line, the largest possible target is presented. As you move forward towards your opponent, the frontal area of the target is reduced. If the opposing attacker approaches goal from an angle the target is also reduced and if, in either case, you advance toward him you can block his view of the goal almost completely. But the following calculated risks are involved:

1. If you don't advance, the attacking forward has the greatest target area at which to aim.

2. If you advance too far too quickly, the attacking player who has the ball may pass to another of his teammates.

3. If you advance too far, the attacking player may attempt to chip or lob the shot over your head. The further you advance the easier this becomes.

4. If you advance too quickly and without control and balance you make it easy for the attacking player to dribble the ball round you and into goal.

If the attacking player is running very fast, his control over the ball may not be too good. In this situation a quick advance by the goalkeeper may enable him to fall on the ball before the attacking player can regain control.

The high volley, or "punt,"
kick is one of the best means of
clearing the ball far downfield.

The proper procedure for long-ball, javelin-type throw.

The over-hand toss *(left)* or side-arm toss *(right)* is used for throws to teammates.

As is the case with all defenders, a good goalie will attempt to "jockey" an attacker, who is bearing down on goal, into the least dangerous position. If you know that the attacker is leftfooted, you'll advance in such a way as to attempt to force him to move right, into a position where he has to try a shot with his weaker foot. You may also feint to rush forward and instead move back, trying to slow the attacker down or make him change his mind. This may allow time for one of your defenders to recover and make a challenge.

Corner and Free Kicks   Corner and free kicks present special positioning problems. For instance, when a corner kick is about to be taken the goalkeeper should stand near the far post of his goal (about two-thirds of the way across the goal mouth), ready to move quickly across his goal or run out to catch a center. His two fullbacks stand near the uprights ready to protect the goal as the goalie moves out. More on the goaltender's role in corner kicks is given on page 147.

When a free kick is to be taken against the defending side (from near the edge of the area), a barrier of three, four, or five players is formed to help block the goal from a direct shot. The wall of players must cover the area of the goal directly in front of the goal with the goalkeeper

The New York Cosmos' first goal was scored by Siggy Stritzl *(extreme left)* over Washington Darts' wall on a curving banana shot.

standing at the other side of the goal. In this way, he can see the ball and be ready to move across the goal to intercept a lobbed shot. The number of players in the human wall varies according to the distance from the goal and the angle of the shot. Incidentally, it is the goalkeeper's decision as to whether or not he wants a wall to protect him on a free kick; but we know of only a few occasions where a goalie has refused the help of a wall from his teammates.

GOALKEEPING SUMMARY

The goalkeeper should remember these six basic rules:

1. Always move toward the ball to gain possession.
2. Always use both hands to catch the ball; and when unable to do so, punch the ball well clear of the mouth of the goal, either upfield or over the goal line for a corner kick.
3. Try to get your body behind the ball whenever possible, and hold the ball against the body when it's caught.
4. When diving at a forward's feet to block the ball, always dive across them and not straight at them (this protects more of the goal and also helps to prevent head injuries).
5. Use caution in throwing or kicking the ball to a teammate; always be on the lookout for interception by an opponent.

When the goalkeeper stays
close to the goal line *(left)*
he leaves a much greater area to shoot
at than when he moves out and cuts
down the shooting angle *(right)*.

6. Tell the other defenders of your intentions so that they can adjust to the situation.

Despite the fact that the goalkeeper is usually less active than his teammates:

1. He must be very fit and extremely agile, with good positional sense. He should concentrate on exercises to quicken his reactions and to strengthen his hands, arms, and shoulders.

2. He must learn when to advance from his goal line to meet an opponent about to shoot, how far to advance, and at what angle he should advance in relation to the goal to make it equally difficult for the opponent to score either by shooting past him or by lifting the ball over his head.

3. He must analyze his own ability to retain possession when challenged in a crowded goal-mouth situation or when diving at full stretch. If in doubt, he should kick, punch, or guide the ball clear of the goal—even at the expense of a corner kick against his team.

4. He must assume the team's field generalship. That is, the goalie should direct the defense. Like a catcher in baseball, he should always be talking and always directing. He should be alerting his teammates to dangerous situations. By his guidance of his defend-

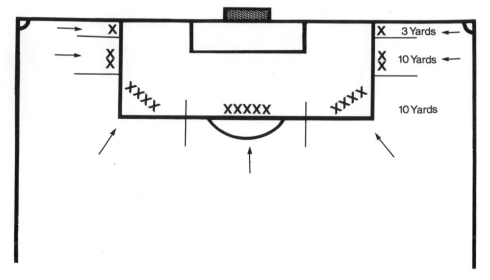

Various wall arrangements used by the Cosmos on free kicks.

ers, the shooting opportunities for the opposing attackers are greatly limited, and he makes things easier for himself. Commands should be given loudly, clearly, and with authority. An indecisive and silent goaltender creates many problems for defenders counting on him for guidance.

Goalkeepers require individual attention in practice sessions and coaches should use the other players to provide realistic shooting and defending situations to give them fully rounded experience. Also, since goalkeepers are sometimes, and for long periods, observers only, they have great opportunity to gain and retain a great deal of knowledge about opposing players' techniques and skills.

Team Play and Systems of Play

SOCCCER is to football what traditional jazz is to classical music. In football, as in classical music, every player knows every note and every move, and everything he is supposed to do: he is playing to a written score, to a written plan. Soccer is like traditional jazz in that the players know the tune that is to be played, know there are an infinite number of varieties as to how to strike a note or a chord—or a play. Both players —jazz or soccer—go out there for a set number of minutes to perform that piece of music, or that game, to the best of their ability as it hits them at the exact moment that they are doing it.

A quarterback, or a classical music conductor, knows before he raises his arms, which may hold a football or a baton, exactly what he is going to do with it and exactly what his players should be doing. In soccer, the players know they are trying to score a goal or trying to stop someone else from scoring a goal; but all during the time the soccer player has the ball at his feet he hasn't one plan to follow. He has many options, depending upon how well his teammates run into position, which way they are in position, how far upfield they are, and whether in that running and taking up of position the defensive team covers them. While there are certain set plays, the majority of soccer is played to a basic team work. The coach instills a certain kind of play into a team, but apart from following that basic pattern, the player who has the ability has the choice of many things to do at any given time on the field. Therefore, we think: football/classical music; soccer/traditional jazz.

In fact one of the many reasons why soccer is attractive both to American players and spectators is this freedom of movement. Attack and defense flow naturally into each other and players can be almost completely unrestricted in their movements. The game, then, is basically a free game, but as in all team games, the aim of a team must be to win the contest. This inevitably means the coordination of eleven individual efforts into a combined team effort—which demands some planning and purpose.

SYSTEMS OF PLAY

A system of play, or team formation, as it is sometimes called, is a recognizable pattern of play resulting from the use of certain players in clearly defined responsibilities on the field. Systems of play must be sufficiently elastic to enable the individual strengths of players to be used to the maximum effect and, also, to allow temporary changes to take place according to the problems which may be caused by opposing team tactics. For instance, suppose a team is playing 3-2-5 system (as described in Chapter 2, this means three fullbacks, two midfielders, and five attackers) and it's the tactic of the attacking team to have their striker penetrate deep and link up with his own center midfield player, leaving the two outside linkmen to work as twin attackers. This means that the defending center-fullback would have two men to cope with, a situation which results in an unfavorable defensive position. To overcome the problem, the system of play would be altered—most likely to 4-2-4 formation—to meet the attacking threat. It is important to remember that the formation indicates only the *main* functions of each player. As has been stated before, everyone must be prepared to play another's position, even if only for a second or two.

Throughout soccer's long history, many ways have been employed to deploy the eleven players. In fact, over the years, the goalkeeper's position is about the only one that hasn't changed its function to any great extent. In the early nineteenth century, teams lined up in a manner such as this:

X

X

XXXXXXXXX

That is, a goalkeeper, one defender, and nine attackers.

By the early twentieth century, it was recognized that defense was equally as important as attack, and the 2-3-5 formation came into general use. This was the period in history when soccer became a world-wide sport, and therefore everyone became familiar with:

```
                              1
                         GOALKEEPER
           2                                                3
     RIGHT FULLBACK                                    LEFT FULLBACK
           4                     5                          6
     RIGHT HALFBACK        CENTER HALFBACK          LEFT HALFBACK
          7            8           9           10           11
       OUTSIDE      INSIDE      CENTER       INSIDE       OUTSIDE
        RIGHT       RIGHT       FORWARD       LEFT         LEFT
```

The 2-3-5 system.

1. The names of the positions on a soccer team.

2. The numbers on players' shirts identifying their positions on the team.

While the position numbering system is no longer used on the back of players' shirts, numbers are still used to describe tactical formations or systems of play. Thus, the 2-3-5 formation meant 2 defenders, 3 midfielders, and 5 attackers. The position of goalkeeper, as previously mentioned, is omitted—he is always in the same position on every team —but all soccer numbering systems progress from the defenders to the midfield players to the attackers.

The 2-3-5 system of play is seldom, if ever, used in modern soccer.

As described in detail in Chapter 8, most teams today used either man-to-man or zone defense coverage. In the former, each player on a team must be responsible for dealing with his opposite number. The goalkeepers are thought to cancel themselves out, since they are only remotely concerned with free play over the field as a whole. The latter type of defense is based on zone or space and, provided that a team can command a zone effectively, the problems of the opposing players need not be too difficult to cope with.

With a 2-3-5 system, the use of either defense meant that the two fullbacks had to look after five attackers. Even if the three linkmen dropped back to help their outnumbered defense, the formation shaped itself into two parallel lines with a large gap in between. Since a gap makes accurate interpassing most difficult, this system is seldom employed, but many publications—including the United States Soccer Football Association's latest rulebook—still illustrate it as soccer's prime formation.

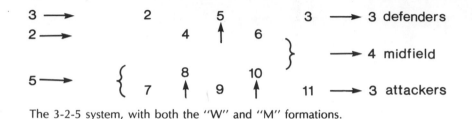

The 3-2-5 system, with both the "W" and "M" formations.

THE 3-2-5 SYSTEM

In 1925, with the introduction of the present international offside rule, the 3-2-5, or w-m, formation was developed in England and soon was employed, with slight variations, by most of the world's teams. As shown here, while there are five attackers listed, the two inside forwards (numbers 8 and 10) play in midfield with the two linkmen (numbers 4 and 6). That is, the "w" shape is the attacking formation, while the "m" is designed for the defense. Many beginning soccer players and fans are slightly confused at first, because although the system is known as the 3-2-5, the responsibilities of the players are such that there are 3 defenders, 4 in the midfield, and 3 attackers.

The key to the success of the 3-2-5 formation is the two inside forwards who have to have both defensive and offensive abilities. Along with the two outside linkmen, they are the "engine room" of both defense and attack. The three-man striking unit (the outside forwards and the striker) are basically the scoring punch, while the three backs are essentially physical players whose strength and size counted for a great deal. While the 3-2-5 system is still employed by teams in some of soccer's low classifications, most professionals and nationals have passed it by.

THE 4-2-4 SYSTEM

In the 1960's, this system gained world-wide popularity and, with various modifications, it is used by most professionals. It employs a four-man defensive unit, a two-man midfield unit, and a four-man attacking unit. In midfield the link between attack and defense is established by the linkmen. When the opposing team has the ball, they retreat quickly to become defensive players. When their own team has possession of the ball, they both become supporting inside forwards. In a rigid form this system of play demands a very high work rate from

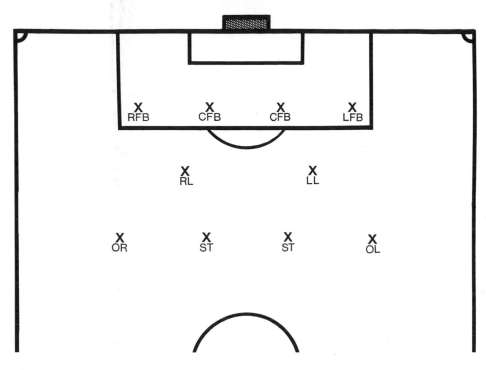

The 4-2-4 system.

the two midfield or link players, who in all phases of the game work in close support of each other.

The basic idea of the 4-2-4 system is to enable a side to have at least six attacking players when in possession of the ball and at least seven defensive players when the opponents have possession. Tactical variations take place to an increasing extent. In many countries the defensive formation involves a double bank of four defenders.

In any system of play, attacking soccer can be emphasized by sending players from deep or midfield positions to support play, or indeed to press home the attack. The use of surprise moves is an integral part of successful attacking soccer, but it involves risk. Risk is calculated on the basis of the understanding which exists between all the players on a team and, naturally, the state of any particular game. The 4-2-4 is a balanced formation giving an equal spread of players over the playing area and an equal division between defense and attack.

THE 4-3-3 SYSTEM

This is one of the more popular modifications of the 4-2-4 system and is a more defense-minded formation. It occurs when a team uses

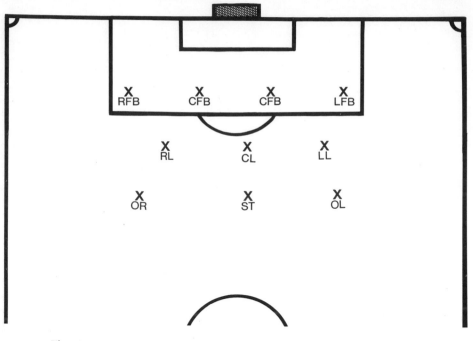

The 4-3-3 system.

the double center-backs and supports this with a unit of three midfield players. These three linkmen form the first line of the defense and also suppport the three attackers at all times. Attacking play can be emphasized by allowing the three midfield players to take part in attacking movements and also by encouraging each of the four backs to break out from defense in support of attacking play whenever they see the opportunity.

As we stated earlier in this chapter, situations often dictate changes in formations. And sometimes these situations are not always caused by play on the field. In the latter part of the 1972 season, the NASL, with permission from FIFA, decided to experiment with the offside rule and hoped that, by changing the offside point from the centerline (see page 201) to the eighteen-yard (penalty) line, goal scoring would increase. But most of the NASL teams switched from their normal 4-2-4 formation to the 4-3-3. Results of the experiment showed that while offside call arguments decreased slightly, goal scoring decreased, and the rule change was dropped.

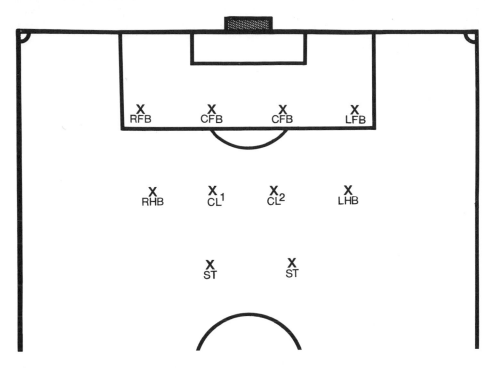

The 4-4-2 system.

When the NASL coaches found that the offside line was only 18 yards from their goal, they also learned that it was more important to have a linkman with good defense ability than a striker. Thus, most of them changed from their conventional formation to a slightly more defensive one due to a situation created in the front offices of the League.

In 1973, again to attempt to increase scoring, an offside "blue line" at 35 yards from the goal line has been employed.

THE 4-4-2 SYSTEM

In this there are only two strikers, but the four linkmen act as the attacking unit. The work demanded from the link players is heavy if the system is a rigid one. Where players are basically competent in most aspects of the game it is possible to share the load from time to time by developing an interchange in function between the linkmen and the two attackers. In the same way, the more advanced of the two center-backs can occasionally see an opportunity to support or exploit an attacking possibility.

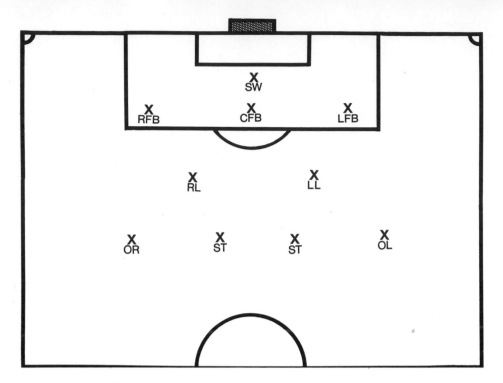

The 1-3-2-4 system.

THE 1-3-2-4 SYSTEM

This system—used primarily in Italy—employs a "sweeper," three defensive backs, two midfield players and four attackers. The sweeper is a defensive player whose task is to collect any balls that come through the back defensive line. To be a sweeper, a player must be able to "read" the movements of the attacking team and must be able to time his runs almost perfectly.

THE 1-4-1-4 SYSTEM

This system employs a sweeper, four defense players, one linkman, and four attackers. The 1-4-1-4 is basically a defensive formation and this aspect is emphasized when the center-backs and fullbacks are restricted to a defensive function. This happens, for example, when the five defenders never, or seldom, advance beyond the half-way line. Here the attacking line operates without any support from the rear other than that which can be offered by the attacking line itself. To fill the gap between defense and attack, one or two strikers have to take up positions behind the remainder—which of course means that the

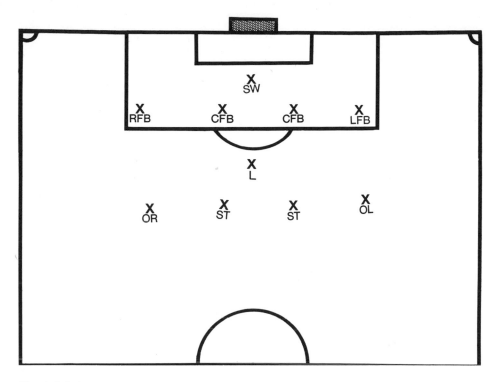

The 1-4-1-4 system.

likelihood of penetration is still further reduced. When this system is used, the midfield player frequently is supported by one or more of the four defensive men. There is no reason why the fullbacks should not also involve themselves in attacking movements, since they will frequently find themselves in advanced positions.

When using one of the systems employing four defensive backs, some teams were unable to break completely with tradition, and certain positions still retained the numbers designated to them at the turn of the century. In many European teams, however, positions are being numbered in various ways, one of which is shown in the diagram here. However, the system is still 4-2-4.

TEAM PLAYERS AND SYSTEMS OF PLAY

Now let's take a look at individual requirements and skills of the three categories of players: defenders, linkmen, and attackers.

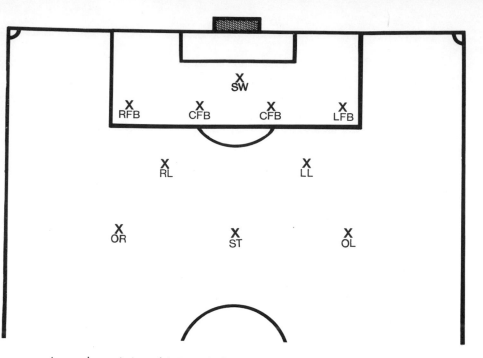

A popular variation of 1-4-1-4 is the new 1-4-2-3 system. This system employs a sweeper, four defenders, two linkmen, and three attackers.

DEFENDERS

The basic techniques that must be developed by a defender are:

1. The ability to kick strongly with both feet.

2. To head the ball strongly up and away from danger, and not to the feet of an opponent.

3. To tackle an opponent without fear of body contact in order to win possession of the ball. A defender must be able to time his runs almost perfectly.

4. To "read" attacking players' moves in order to intercept passes.

5. To gain control of the ball quickly.

6. To be able to concentrate on guarding an opponent rather than following the ball. (Defenders who are ball watchers allow their opponents to sneak into better attacking positions.)

In modern soccer, the defending backs also must know how to score. Over the years, Barry Mahy, our left-back, has scored several vital goals, while in 1972 Werner Roth clipped in with a couple of important assists on goals.

```
                    1
                GOALKEEPER

 2           5           6           3                    1
RIGHT      RIGHT       LEFT        LEFT
BACK      CENTER      CENTER       BACK      2       3           4        5

             4          10                          6               7
           RIGHT       LEFT
          LINKMAN    LINKMAN          8       9              10       11

 7           8           9          11
RIGHT      RIGHT       LEFT        LEFT
WINGER     CENTER     CENTER      WINGER
```

The numbering system used in a standard 4-2-4 *(left)*. Many European teams follow the new numbering arrangement shown at the right. The system is still 4-2-4.

LINKMEN

The following qualities are found in a good midfield player:

1. The ability to work hard but conserve energy to use to the best advantage of the team.

2. The ability to defend against the opposing midfield players by tackling with determination, and/or positioning shrewdly and harassing opponents to limit their opportunities and thus force errors.

3. The ability to anticipate the change of possession of the ball and change from an attacking to a defending role, or vice versa, before the opposing midfield players.

4. The ability to seek good positions in which to receive the ball from the defenders and provide accurate passing service to his attackers. And the ability to find good supporting positions to help them out of trouble.

5. The skill to dribble out of a difficult situation when not supported by teammates, and the ability to see the opportunity to shoot at goal.

6. The individual skill to retain possession of the ball when unsupported against heavy pressure and hard tackling from an opponent.

7. Be alert. Expect defensive mistakes. Be ready to shoot on sight, make quick decisions, and watch for a shot or pass. A numerical advantage in defense or attack can be obtained by the linkman who anticipates a change of possession.

A good outside forward like the Cosmos' Josef Jelinek must be able to set up an attacking play.

It helps to have a powerful physique to withstand the physical contact. Linkmen must be able to do everything, for they are both defenders and attackers. Actually, it was because of our linkmen—Siggy Stritzl, Johnny Kerr, and Dieter Zajdel—that we were able to switch from our 4–2–4 to the more defensive 4–3–3 formation without losing any of our offensive punch when there was a rule change. In fact, Dieter scored our only goal in our 2–1 defeat, in 1972, by the Moscow Dynamo.

ATTACKERS

Players in attacking positions require the following abilities:

1. The individual skill and speed to beat an opposing defender.
2. The determination to keep trying despite being subject to strong body contact and despite experiencing failure through continuously losing the ball to opponents or shooting wide.
3. The ability to quickly assess the right proportion of individualism and combination play with other teammates.
4. The ability to assess the weaknesses of opponents.

5. The ability to shoot hard, pass accurately, and, particularly as center striker, the ability to head the ball with accuracy and power.

6. A sense of anticipation of teammates' moves in order to gain extra yardage on his opponents.

7. Skill at chipping the ball to attackers in the goal mouth.

8. The ability to beat defenders using speed, dribbling skills, and wall passes.

Speed off the mark is an essential asset of all attackers. Their ball control, pass accuracy, and particularly their skill at screening must be exceptional.

BASIC TEAM TACTICS

There are three principal phases of the game:

1. Attack
2. Defense
3. Preparation, or midfield play

In the third phase neither team has established a complete domination of play, but is involved in re-organization before building up its defense or making an attack. Of course, whenever a team loses possession of the ball, all the players on the team must think defensively. Obviously, some will be immediately committed defensively, either in covering the opponents closely, withdrawing in order to provide a solid final line of defense, or actually challenging opposing players for possession. Similarly, when a team has possession of the ball, every member of that team thinks positively about attack. It may be, for example, that the left-fullback finds himself remote from play when his own outside-right forward has the ball in the far corner of the field. He may move much nearer to his opposing striker, thus taking himself away from a central covering position. He does so with two possibilities in mind: if play switches to his side of the field, he can move quickly in support; also, he has tightened his covering so that if his team loses possession of the ball the opposing team will not have unrestricted scope for passing.

The first and most important principle in soccer, as we have mentioned several times, is that ball possession determines everything. There are times when risking losing possession is justified by an opportunity to shoot at goal. The closer it is pressing its opponents' penalty area, the more a team is justified in taking such a chance. On the other hand, the nearer a team is to its own penalty area, the fewer should be the risks taken. Accuracy and confident control of the ball are basic requirements of players—particularly when they gain possession of the ball in defensive positions.

Let's look at how a team personnel will affect a team's tactics.

Suppose that our outside forwards are quite capable of beating opponents with the ball but are not overly fast runners. Tactically, we should modify our system of play to make the most of these players' skills with the ball and to disguise their lack of speed. Long passes over the opposing fullbacks would be a waste of time except where the outside attackers have tempted the fullbacks into positions remote from their goal. These long passes would be made into the space behind their backs for one of the strikers to run into.

During attacking phases of the game we may decide that the outside forward can be used to the greatest advantage nearest opponents' penalty area. If we're able to pass the ball to them in wide positions in this part of the field we may be able to create a situation where they can use their dribbling to beat the opposing fullbacks and so to turn the flanks of the defense. In this part of the field we may ask our other attackers to deliberately move away from the outside forwards in order to draw away covering defenders. Also, we may find that one of our forwards has an ability to beat a fullback by going outside him or "down the line." Where this is so we need to ensure that the path down the line is clear of other players.

During a game we should read certain aspects of the opposing team's play. The general pattern should be recognized and, after a while, the styles of individual players noted. Tactically, we must exploit their weaknesses. For instance, one of the opposing linkmen may be inclined to get drawn out to the wing. When the outside forward obtains the ball, the left linkman, for example, tends to challenge him if he is near enough. An attempt to exploit this weakness might involve our central strikers moving out to extreme wing positions both behind and in front of the outside-right.

Frequently, it is difficult to spot weaknesses in an opposing side, and it may then be necessary to direct our attention to their strongest aspects of play. A team is confident in doing the things it can do well. To play on the strength of a team is to try to encourage it to become overconfident.

Let's consider ourselves up against players who show themselves to be a strong attacking side. Individually and collectively they are quick and accurate, and possess clever dribblers; also, they can shoot. We

A great goalkeeper save stops a Cosmos' shot from entering the goal.

might decide to encourage them to attack by falling back or retreating to the edge of our penalty area where we set up a defensive structure of seven or eight players. Our aim is to draw more and more of the opposing players into attacking movements. Our defensive aim is to restrict the amount of free space within our defense and to restrict the movement of attacking players behind us. When a side is heavily committed to attack, it is most vulnerable to counterattack, since there is the maximum amount of space behind the rearmost defenders.

To encourage heavy attacking play we might ask both our inside forwards to adopt deep defensive positions in order to encourage the opposing linkmen into advanced attacking movements. If the ball can now be played from defense we have established possession of the ball in a four-against-four situation where our strikers are opposed by their defensive line. If our strikers can support each other quickly a rapid breakthrough may be achieved.

One of the most important aspects of tactical development involves establishing a numerical advantage. In defense or attack, a team must aim at having at least one extra man. In attack this will mean that however tight the marking by opposing defenders, one man is free to support or press home the advantage. It may be that the numerical superiority means only a brief moment in time and a small space in which two attackers are able to interpass and beat one defender. It may be established during a full attacking movement which is supported from a deep defensive position: for example, a fullback may suddenly join in an advanced attacking movement. In defense, the extra man may be involved in deflecting the opposing attack across the field to less dangerous areas, or he may be responsible for covering gaps rather than marking specific opposing players.

Whatever the phase of the game a numerical advantage should be the aim, and once it has been established its exploitation depends upon one thing alone: accuracy in passing. It has often been said that if a player can't pass accurately and with control he can't really play soccer. The ability to direct a pass exactly where it is intended to go, at the right speed, with just enough spin or swerve, if required, is of major importance to all players—from the goalkeeper to the outside-left. Where we are concerned with the exploitation of numerical superiority what we are really concerned with is the establishment and exploitation of a two-against-one situation.

Whenever a player receives the ball he should have already assessed the situation around him and he should have made a selection from the passing opportunities available. In this way he tries to be one, two, or three moves ahead all the time. He may receive the ball during rapid changes of play and much movement of players around him. In these "tight" situations he may not have time to make accurate and controlled judgments. Obviously, then, if he has one teammate to whom he can pass he has no choice; if he has three or four the position is simplified. These choices can only be possible if teammates move towards, rather than away from, the player towards whom the ball is being played. One often hears the expression "they had the luck or the run of the ball." It is only possible for a team to have the run of the ball if that team has sufficient players there to whom the ball can run. This movement of supporting players towards the man with the ball achieves two things. It simplifies his choice of passing possibilities and also draws opponents in the same direction. This in itself assists the player with the ball.

A team which plays controlled, methodical soccer will often employ deliberate passing movements which appear to have little or no purpose so far as scoring goals is concerned. They may deliberately interpass to draw opponents towards the ball. They do this in order to create for a through-pass towards their opponents' goal. The higher the soccer classification the more a team must use setting-up play to tempt the opposing team into making mistakes.

7

A Team on Attack

THE object of an attack is the object of the game of soccer: the scoring of goals. To score goals, a team must usually outwit their opponents' defense. And this usually requires luring the defense into so-called "dangerous" positions before the decisive movements on the goal can be made. Soccer teams have various offensive formations and play patterns that they try to follow, much in the same manner that a football team sets up passing or running plays or formations, but a team which limits its attacking approach to one or two methods will have serious problems if these fail. And, of course, any tactical attacking plans must be suited to the ability of the players on the team.

For instance, if all the forward unit on a team are small, quick players, the attacking plan should be to pass accurately, rapidly, and close to the ground. On the other hand, if a team has a burly striker, his ability to make hard passes in the middle of the field can be employed in two ways.

First, a tall, strong striker can be used as a "wall," by "bouncing" the ball off him to get past an opponent. His team member hits the ball hard at him and keeps running. "The wall" turns the ball sideways. The defender who has gone in to challenge him is left stranded. Then the teammate regains the ball and goes on to shoot. The second way of employing the striker's height and strength is by sending high passes into the goal area, so he can head at the goal.

As stated earlier, the Cosmos' favorite attacking formation is a four-man attack force with two linkmen backing them up. Our outside-right forward, Josef Jelinek, as previously noted, is one of hardest, most accurate shooters in the NASL. Our striker, Randy Horton, is one of the tallest and strongest men in the league and we use him as a big man

Randy Horton is the leading scorer of the New York Cosmos. Here he heads in a goal against the St. Louis Stars.

should be employed. Our other striker during the past year was either Willie Mfum or Everald Cummings. Both men are very fast and skillful shots close to the goal. Our outside-left forward was Jorge Siega, also one of the fastest and most accurate shooters in the league. And when Jorge broke his leg in mid-season, Roby Young filled in to give us one of the most balanced attacking units in North America.

Our basic formations, as with any professional team, are not meant to be rigidly maintained throughout the entire game: the way in which an attack develops will alter the positions of players in relation to each other. In fact, in modern attacking play, the interchange of player positions is one of the best ways to upset the coverage of the opposing defense. For example, when an outside forward is in possession of the ball, the striker may move away from the center of the field and run ahead of the outside man, ready to receive a pass down the wing. The other striker then moves into the center position, and one of the linkmen takes up his position. If the players are capable of changing their style of play to fit their new positions, this type of switch can

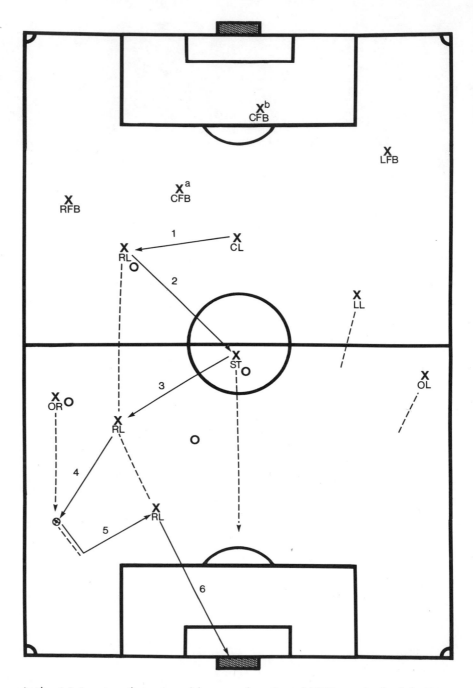

In the 4-3-3 system that we used for a good portion of 1972 season, the linkmen played a very important part in our offensive punch. As shown here, our right linkman on the sixth offensive move has a shot on goal.

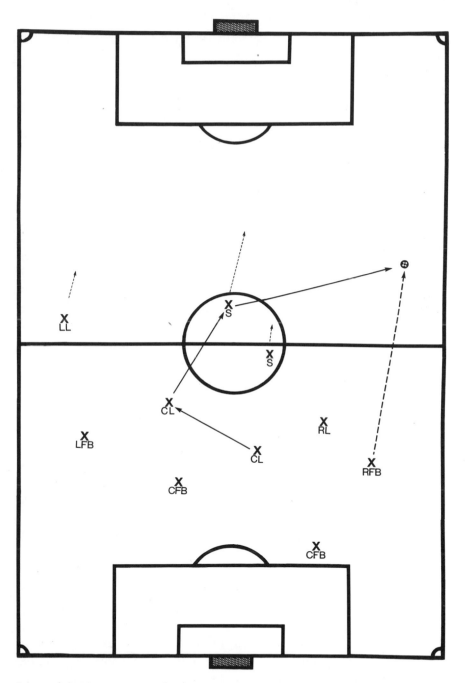

Even a defensive system such as a 4-4-2 (four defenders, four linkmen, and two strikers) can be offensive, as shown here, by bringing the right-fullback up into an outside-right forward position.

considerably upset a defense. There is always a danger, however, that players may become so absorbed in weaving patterns that they lose sight of the purpose of attack: to score goals.

BUILDING AN ATTACK

As you'll see in Chapter 8, modern defensive play is highly organized. While the organizers of soccer—as well as those in baseball, football and basketball—have tried to legislate offense into the game, all attempts to do so have failed. It seems that the only way to increase scoring opportunities is to set up better methods of attack. This is easier stated than accomplished.

A defending team is waiting for mistakes; it may, at the same time, actively encourage the opposing side to make them. Most defensive formations, provided that there is a clear understanding of priorities of their functions, can be simple and yet extremely effective in their simplicity. This can be easily proven by allowing six to eight players to attack a goal which at times is defended by only four or five players. In many instances the number of scoring shots will be very low, indeed the number of shooting attempts may even be few. This is because an attack which is within reach of goal demands precision and skill, while the defense is simply concerned with stopping the attack: their task demands a great deal less accuracy and they can merely kick the ball out of play—a non-skillful tactic but most effective.

In any attacking formations, too much organization can be most restrictive. As players are faced with the problems created by a defense, they must be permitted to try to solve them individually. True, they should have a basic attacking plan determined by their coach, and the team may well have "set," or practiced, plays, but the players should be encouraged to react naturally and intelligently to new problems.

Let's suppose that our team has decided that its attacking strength is in the ability of our forward to beat the opposing fullbacks on the outside. Our basic attacking plan might be to isolate opposing fullbacks, leaving the outside forward to attack the fullback one-on-one. Crossfield passes might also be employed from the strikers or linkmen to try to use the forward's speed. This is good, as an attacking plan, but in a game one of the forwards may find that he's more easily able to beat the fullback on the inside. If this is so the attack must be adaptable enough to exploit this alternative possibility.

To overcome a well organized defense, the attack must be kept in continuous motion—this means even the players without the ball, since motion will confuse the defense and will create open passing situations. And, since the defenders will have to decide whether to maintain their field position or play the attackers more closely, this usually puts the attack in full control. This constant motion and keeping the ball in play is one of the main reasons for the success of the Cosmos attack and why we get so many goal shots.

One of the most important skills which any player can have is the ability to take on and beat an opponent with the ball. Whenever and wherever you can beat an opponent you have successfully created problems for the opposing defense. You have established a position where the attacking side has a spare man—yourself! And to accomplish this, you must keep your opponents constantly guessing.

For example, when dribbling, there are several positive moves you can perform that may confuse a defender who is chasing or facing you for the ball.

—When hard-pressed in a chase, try making a sudden move—even leave the ball two steps behind—then go get it again when your opponent backs up.

—Another trick to relieve pressure in a close situation is to point your finger at a teammate and fake a pass to him.

In the final attacking stage of the game—just inside and outside your opponents' penalty area—your ability to dribble and beat an opposing defender is of great value. This is a part of the field where defenders must tackle with care, since a careless tackle can result in the award of a penalty kick. It follows, therefore, that players who are gifted in their ability to dribble around an opponent should reserve this ability in the main for that part of the field where it is likely to be most effective: to show all one's tricks in midfield is to give opposing players too much information.

DEPTH ON THE ATTACK

Ideally, an attack will move smoothly, with flexibility and teamwork, from one end of the field to the other. There's a tendency for the players taking part in a concerted attacking movement, however, to flatten out the shape of their formation as they approach their opponent's penalty area. Those in front are slowed up in their attacking moves by the danger of offside, or by having to stop to collect the ball, while those coming up from behind race too far forward once they have passed the ball. A straight line of attack considerably increases the chances of losing the ball, since the number of possibilities is greatly reduced and whatever passing possibilities that do exist in a flat attack, square passing, or passing across the field must increase. When square passing increases the risk of a pass being intercepted increases. In most cases the defenders are well positioned to step into the intervening spaces to intercept the ball, and the attackers will then have little chance of retrieving it. Also, the players can be put into an offside position without too much difficulty. When an attacking team moves upfield with reasonable depth in its formation, there's a great deal more opportunity of finding open spaces in which to interpass and maneuver the ball.

As illustrated here, the left linkman has the ball and the attacking unit has taken up flat or straight-line positions relative to each other, and presumably, are closely covered. But if two of the attackers were to move towards the left linkman (see bottom illustration), they would increase the passing possibilities open to him and at the same time present difficulties to the defenders who might be covering them too closely. The decision for the defenders, is, of course, whether or not to follow the attackers. If they follow their attackers they permit space to be formed behind them which can be exploited by the left linkman's utilization of a through-pass. If they remain in covering positions, the opposing attack is permitted a great deal more freedom to press home its attacking formation. (Obviously, when there is real doubt in their minds, the defenders won't be drawn into following the attacking players.)

From the coach's point of view in the NASL, the minimum number of players which can produce depth in attack must be three, and as a rule they'll find themselves in some sort of triangular formation, although the nature of the triangle will frequently change and change rapidly. The three-man attacking formation illustrated here, for instance, shows the outside-left forward, left linkman and left striker attacking in depth. This attack may develop in such a way that the left linkman spots an opportunity to move into an advanced position. One of the other players will balance the left linkman's forward run to continue to provide depth, as shown. Here the left striker has tried to tempt the center-fullback away from his position to open up a path for forward runs of the left linkman, and, having done this, he has swung around in behind the other attackers as a supporting player. But the shape of formation—whether it resembles a triangle, diamond, square, M, or W—is not overly important; what is vital is that it has depth and never flattens out to a straight line.

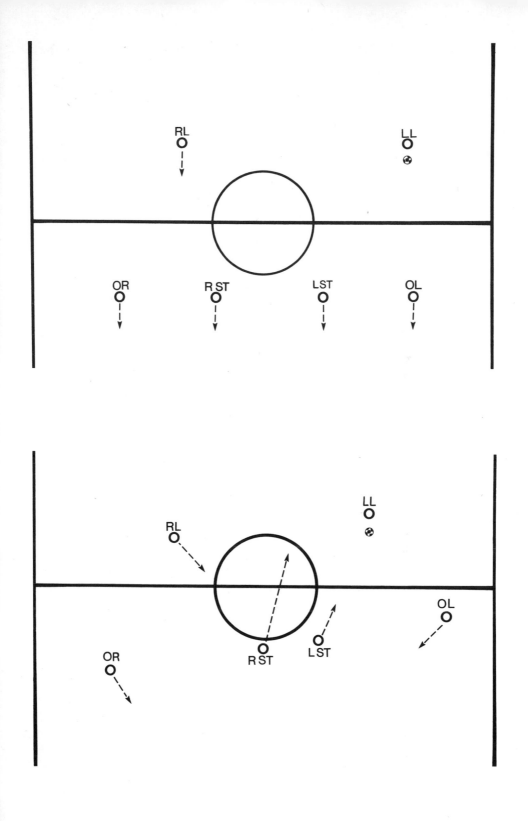

DIRECTION OF AN ATTACK

Defense, as we'll learn in Chapter 8, is primarily concerned with reducing the amount of space through which and into which passes can be made, and also with restricting the range of area in which attacking players can move. In order to create necessary attacking space, the direction of the attack must be changed often and rapidly. In other words, as the forward attacks "in depth," the players should maneuver the ball in both forward and backward directions. These shuttle passes up and down the field are most difficult for the defense to cope with. In fact, one of the most effective passes preceding a shot on goal is the ball which is turned back to a teammate coming up from behind. The back, or reverse, pass enables the approaching player to adjust his movement to correct any error in the direction of the pass. Because he's moving forward at speed, he can kick the ball as hard as required, and, since he's facing play, he is in excellent position for the shot.

The back pass comes in handy at other times, too. For example, when tightly covered by the defense and you feel that a forward pass might be intercepted, it would be wise to stop your run and make a short backward pass to a teammate. Then he can start another attack pattern and you can move to an area where the attacking can be reopened. But make sure that back or sideways passes are short, crisp, and unexpected.

The diagonal pass is one of the most valuable in modern soccer. In the case of the through-pass, the player often moves diagonally as the ball is kicked forward. The success of this pass lies in using it when it is least expected or when the defense is clearly vulnerable to this type of move. It requires considerable accuracy and demands a good sense of judgment, and, when expertly done, can break the defense completely open.

In the less congested area at midfield, passes can be made in front of a player for him to gather in his stride and often at speed. The same type of pass is also necessary in any forceful attacking movement, but the nearer the attacking team is to a massed defense, the less will be the chance of success in making such a pass. Here it becomes vital that the build-up of attacking play is by controlled passes made to the feet of the attackers. Often the receivers of such passes will be in positions with their backs towards their opponents' goal. Remember that passes kicked too hard will be very difficult to control, especially if the recipient is tightly covered. At the same time, the ability to play to the feet

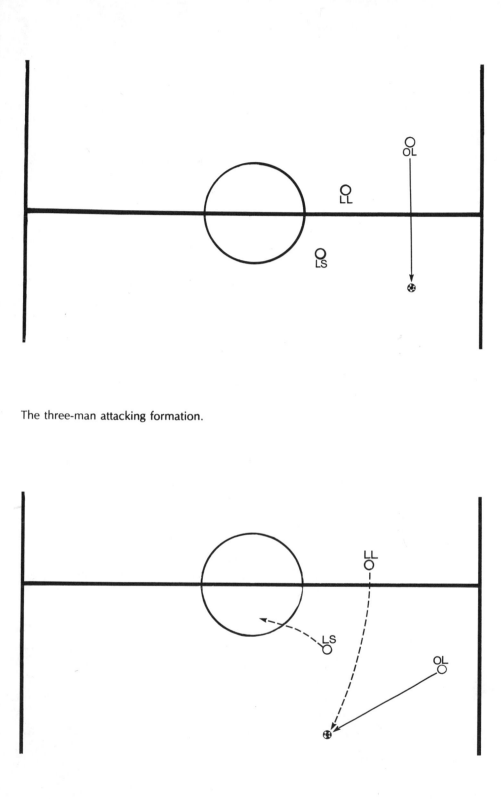

The three-man attacking formation.

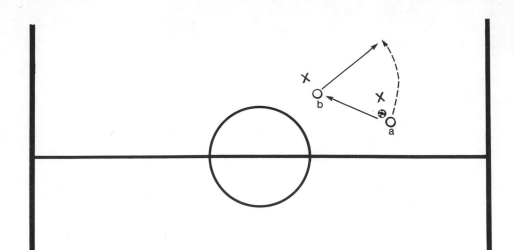

The basic employment of a wall pass.

of tightly covered players is important when close to the goal. If defenders don't cover tightly by moving close to the opposing attacker they may give him time to control the ball and shoot on goal. If the player to whom the ball is played can control it while employing his body as a shield, then there is a possibility for a pass to be kicked or flicked away to oncoming attackers.

Screening is a technique whereby the body is employed to keep the ball from an opponent either when it is in a player's possession or when it comes within playing distance. It is an important skill since it allows you to hold the ball or to hide your intentions so far as passing it is concerned. The pass which is deflected by a player who is screening the ball has been likened to the pass that is returned after kicking a ball against a wall. The angle at which the ball rebounds will vary according to the angle of the pass. This type of pass is frequently employed to exploit a situation where two players are momentarily facing one opponent. Alternatively, as shown here, you can pass the ball to a tightly covered teammate, screening the ball from your opponent, and return it at an angle between the two defenders. Many different uses of the wall pass can be practiced to suit various situations. For instance, as shown at the top, the typical wall pass is given from the left striker to the outside-left forward who runs behind the right-fullback. In the

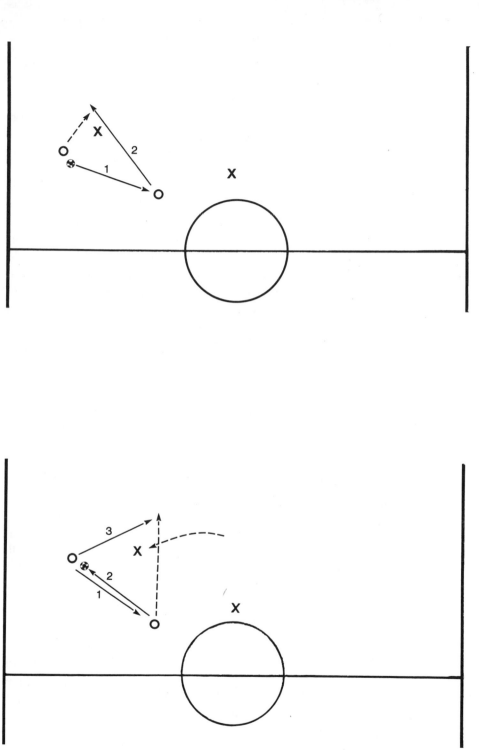

bottom illustration, the right-fullback has moved to cut off this pass and the left striker has given a return pass to the outside-left forward who now acts as the wall. He pushes the ball at an angle behind the fullback for the left striker to run through. An important factor in any successful wall passing technique is that the player who acts as the wall must be in a position where his teammate can make the first pass to him. In addition, the "wall" player should be either standing still or moving sideways towards his teammate; and the wall or return pass should be given first time. The wall pass must be executed quickly but it is most effectively employed when the approach play has been slowed down.

Actually, a change of pace involved in playing the so-called popular open, or long-passing and fast-running, game is that it tends to become a one-pace game. Since fast, long passes have to be done rather quickly, inaccuracy will often occur—as, for example, when attacking players tend to start their attacking runs early to get a head start on opponents. This type of soccer may be exciting to watch, but when accuracy deteriorates the game becomes a shambles. Long passes are extremely vital to good soccer attack play provided they are employed when the possibility for success is at its greatest.

A team which plays a one-pace game consistently quickly attunes the opposing team to its speed. Little or no surprise is possible, since the pace of the game has really no variation. Also, in such a situation attacking players are in a rather difficult position, since they have no time in which to read the developments in play which take place behind them. They know that the ball will be kicked quickly and powerfully and that they must be prepared to run early.

Slowing the pace of the game doesn't necessarily mean that the players would take more time over movements; it *could* result in casual play which can lead to players being caught in possession of the ball and to intercepted passes. Slowing the pace of the game is generally accomplished by taking the direction of play away from your opponents: that is, safe passes are made with no immediately apparent intention of penetrating your opponents' defense. When this is done, there is a number of players near to the ball and therefore any one of these is likely to have time in which to make the penetration pass in a controlled way. Opponents are often deceived into standing still or even into being drawn away from the goal they're defending, and their defensive concentration may lapse. Changing the pace of a game is usually accomplished by linkmen and those behind them. This is a relatively safe part of the field since mistakes can be covered, particularly when four or five players are involved in interpassing.

Defenders are clearly handicapped when they are compelled to pivot round to keep play in view. Not only does the turn slow up their movement, but they can't assess the situation fully if they haven't all the players in view. One method of unbalancing or turning a defense that the Cosmos and most pro teams use is called "crossfield switch play."

All that is involved in the theory of the switch plan of attack is that as the attacking formation shapes on one wing, the defense balances its cover to face a direct thrust from that flank. A quick transference of action to the other side of field "seesaws" the defense and involves it in a considerable readjustment of its position. Switch, or crossfield, play can be started from a number of positions. The goalkeeper should be able to feed either wing at will. Fullbacks and linkmen should be able to employ the pass to the opposite wing. The move is most effective when making a direct attack on goal. For example, the left-fullback, left striker and outside-left forward work a series of short passes and dribbles along the left sideline. This action, of course, will bring an immediate and natural alignment of the defense to this attack challenge which appeared to be a penetration on the left. An unexpected crossfield pass over the heads of the defending players to a teammate on the right side or in the center portion of the field will turn the defense. In that brief moment, while the defense is turning to follow the crossfield pass, the attack pattern is opened to a kick on goal, increased pressure in the goal area, or a return pass through a shaken defense.

When the Cosmos use the switch play, we prefer to have the receiver of the crossfield pass to go into the goal area and take the shot on net. In such cases, he would try a shot as hard and low as possible, or if he were in close enough to the net, just a pop into the corner of the cage. Of course if the goaltender has recovered from the switch action and is properly positioned, a shot toward the upper corners of goal will be the toughest to stop. However, there's no sure shot if the goalkeeper is well positioned. If you have a shot, take it.

The basic premise behind crossfield pass play discloses an important point about any coordinated attack when it is confronted by a competent, well organized defense. A good defender constantly anticipates. If he can determine the next step in the sequence of the attack he is better prepared to cope with it. Speed and excellent ball control may frequently succeed in evading a tackle or an interception, but if a defender can be forced into making a wrong anticipation he is most likely to be beaten.

WIDTH ON THE ATTACK

Since a defense is made stronger by closing its ranks, attackers should employ every means at their disposal to spread defenders out across the full width of the field, especially in the attacking half of the field. But this can only be achieved if the attacking team has passing opportunities over the entire width of the field.

When the defending team is retreating to concentrate on their defense, should the attacking players, particularly on the wings, follow them into the sector of the field just outside the penalty area they'll make this space even more restricted than it is. By having players in wide positions the attack may tempt defending players away from central strong positions. This is especially true if one or more defenders is known to have a liking for physical challenge. Players of this type often take risks in order to be in a position to tackle for the ball; they usually take up positions slightly closer to whichever of the attacking players are in their particular portion of the defensive zone.

But however competent and intelligent a defense may be, and however restrained the individual players within it, human nature still plays a most important part. Any team subjected to the physical and psychological pressure of a sustained attack for a long period of time will tend to become anxious. It should be kept in mind that a defending team can only breathe easily when it succeeds in retaining possession of the ball. The longer the time that a team is without possession the less relaxed and confident they become—and the greater the risks they may be tempted to take. Psychological pressure is a factor which must be taken into consideration in all tactical attacking plans.

PENETRATION OF THE ATTACK

Penetration is the key to scoring goals. A team may indulge in interpassing throughout the entire game without ever posing an immediate threat to the opposing goal. While penetrative play can develop in all phases of the game, the creation of penetration possibilities becomes more difficult the nearer the attacking side approaches the opponents'

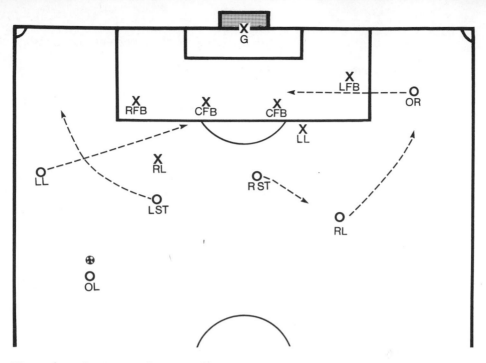

Diagonal running is a good way to obtain space.

goal, since the space available for control and the gaps through which passes can be made diminish all the time.

DIAGONAL RUNNING

A good defense will rarely, if ever, permit attacking players to run unopposed toward goal. The more these long, through-passes are tried, the more a defense will fall back and cover, thus cutting off this possibility. Players on attack who run towards the goal make themselves difficult targets for a pass and also draw defenders in a direction which the defenders are glad to follow. But, as stated earlier in this chapter, one of the best ways to disturb a defense is to continually change the positions of the attacking players. An intelligent defender who is operating against the same opponent in the same part of the field for the entire game has a fairly easy job because he'll learn far more about the attacker's play than the attacker learns about his: this is a natural consequence of the negative side of defensive play. Defenders faced, however, with opponents who continually interchange their positions properly are often confused and, of course, confusion on the part of the defense is the best help an attack can have.

The two methods most commonly used to obtain a good interchange pattern are diagonal running and overlap running. The illustration shows some planned diagonal movements that will often break a well organized and concentrated defense on the edge of their penalty area (the left linkman has the ball): the outside-left forward moves across field to the left-striker position, while the left striker has moved towards the outside position to offer himself as a target for left linkman's pass; it is likely that the left striker could assist by running outside the outside-left; he would then open space for the outside forward should the left linkman desire to pass him. The outside-right forward may have decided to try a diagonal run behind the center-fullback, either for a pass or to create a diversion by drawing attention to himself. The right striker could then run outside the fullback, perhaps taking an opposing central defender with him and also re-establishing wide passing possibilities in attack.

The utilization of diagonal movements accomplishes two objectives of any attacking plan: 1) It shakes the confidence of defenders by surprising them; and 2) it obtains passing space. It is important to remember that all the movements of attacking players near the penalty area have to be watched closely and judged quickly by defenders. They are never quite sure whether attackers are moving to receive a pass or to lure them away from a position in which some other teammate may receive it.

OVERLAPPING RUNS

When a defense is well organized, the defenders are adept at moving just so far to cover attackers and then leaving them to other defenders. They'll also be acutely aware of any attempt to move behind them. Overlapping runs are therefore frequently employed to try to turn the defense. In the diagram on page 139, the defense is able to cover opponents tightly. To produce an overlap the outside-right forward, who is in possession of the ball, moves infield towards the opposing left-fullback. The right striker moves slightly away from the right wing —principally to reduce the cover on that flank. The overlap can then be made by either the right striker, right linkman, or right-fullback running outside the outside-right and down the line. The outside-right can now play the ball down the wing or, if the left-fullback is clever enough to block this possibility, he can try to beat the left-fullback on the inside. If the right striker drops back to cover the pass down the wing, the way is open for the outside-right to move inside. If the right

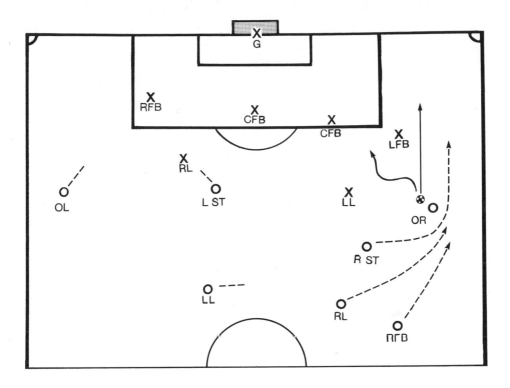

striker attempts to cover this possibility then he must leave the pass down the sidelines as a good possibility.

The use of overlapping runs is a good way of obtaining extra men in tight playing situations and, at the same time, makes for a high degree of penetration in attacking play. The success of this move lies in the fact that opponents don't usually pay that much attention to a supporting player's movement when they're behind the player with the ball.

USE OF THE OPEN SPACE

In the various attacking maneuvers so far discussed, the importance of "open space" has been mentioned. The task of making a good pass is greatly simplified by the wise positioning of the other players. The fact that you may often run into good open spaces and yet not receive the ball doesn't matter. Your movement helps to draw attention away from the actual direction of the attack. It may also create a better opening for a teammate. Players must think ahead so that each time a pass is made they will—directly or indirectly—help the player who is receiving the ball. In fact, movements in which players run into positions to decoy other players from certain parts of the field in order that more effective passes can be made are known as "movements off the ball." The truly intelligent player is constantly aware of the value of such movements. They are vital if a team is to become an effective attacking unit.

When an attack is organized, the players should be running into position even as the ball approaches the player who is going to make the pass. And if he delays the ball, his teammate may have to check and run into other open spaces. After making a pass, you should never stand still: you must be on the move to a new position so that you can receive a return if necessary. For instance, a fullback, after passing the ball back to his goalie, should run into an open space for the return in case the goalkeeper decides to make it to him. After passing the ball to one of his forwards, a linkman should keep himself in close contact, ready to receive a return back-pass should this be necessary. To be eager for the ball in this way demands a high degree of fitness as well as a quick sense of positioning. It opens up numerous possibilities of inter-passing, because each player must ever be striving to improve his position as the attack develops.

SET PLAYS

When compared to football and basketball, soccer has few "set" or "practiced" plays. Most teams work out and practice their own favorite methods of starting or restarting play at the kick-off and at throw-ins, corner kicks and free kicks. It's easier to plan the initial stages of an attack pattern when play begins with a dead ball, since the players usually start from stationary positions: thus the team playing the ball can hide, to some extent, its intentions. But, of course, the opposing team is usually carefully positioned to make a defensive counterattack.

THE KICK-OFF

At the start of the game and of the second half, as well as after each goal, a kick-off is employed. This is the only time when the two teams actually face each other from separate halves of the field, with each player standing in set positions. Prior to the kick-off, players on the non-kicking team must stay at least 10 yards away from the ball.

Unlike football, the kicking team in soccer tries to retain control of

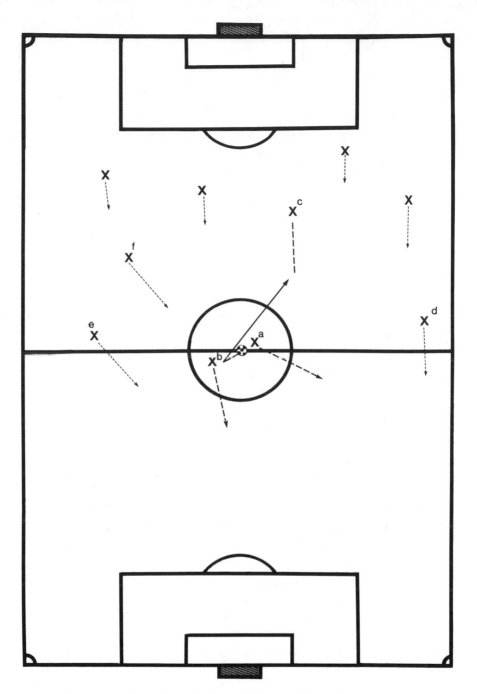

In order to get some depth from the kick-off, Player A kicks off to B, who, in turn, plays the ball backward diagonally to Player C. At the same time, Players D, E, F should move into offensive positions.

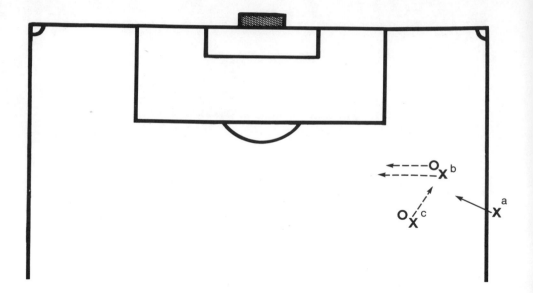

the ball. The kicker has to move the ball forward only 28 inches for it to be in play, but he can't kick it again until at least one other player has touched it. On Cosmos kick-offs, as shown here, our left striker makes a short pass to the right striker, who in turn makes a sharp back-pass to the right linkman. This gives the attacking units time to advance into open spaces. As they run forward they can interchange positions to decoy defenders away from the spot where the attack is to emerge. If successfuly accomplished, there may well be a chance for an immediate attack on goal. This particular kick-off play requires that the pass-back be accurate and well timed. And the receiver, the right linkman, must hold the ball the correct length of time for the attack to get into position.

Another kick-off play that we sometimes use is for the striker to indulge in a quick bout of interpassing to break through the line of the opposing forward units. A long, lobbed pass from the center of the field to a fast-moving outside forward, or to one of the strikers who has moved ahead, may also be effective, especially if the player for whom the pass is intended reaches the last line of the defense at the same instant as the ball.

DROP-BALL

A drop-ball in soccer is equivalent to a face-off in hockey or a jump-ball in basketball. It is called by the referee after a stoppage of play caused

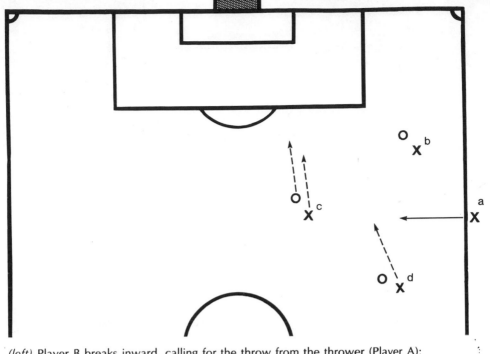

(left) Player B breaks inward, calling for the throw from the thrower (Player A); the defender follows. The thrower withholds the ball, awaiting C to cut into the open space which was created by Player B. (top) Player C breaks forward calling for the ball but doesn't get it. Player D then comes into offensive position in the open space and throws the ball to Player A. Player A attempts to throw it but doesn't, which leaves space for Player D to break in. (bottom) Player C runs in and takes the defender with him, creating space, and bringing Player D, who is in the area, into a position to receive a pass. Player C runs in and calls for the ball. Player A doesn't throw him the ball but holds it and throws it to Player D, who has taken a position in the **space that Player C left**.

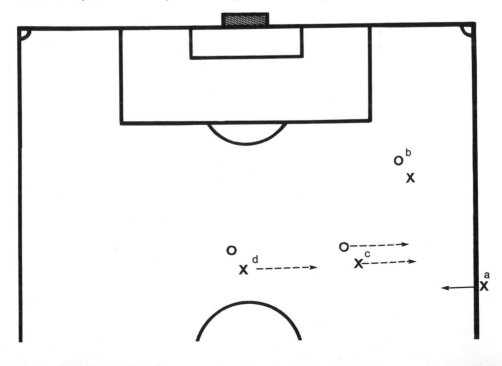

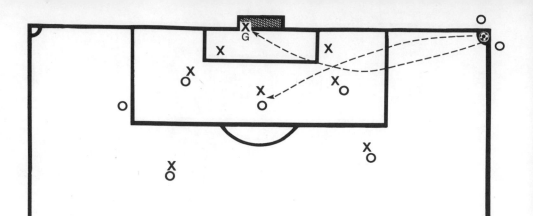

While a straight kick can be used, most outside forwards prefer to use either an inswinger or an outswinger. One is to reach a player away from goal while the other is to get the ball into goal. Since the kick in the illustration is taken from the right corner, the left-foot kick is an inswinger, while the right-foot kick is an outswinger or a straight kick.

by an injured player or some abnormal playing condition—the temporary loss of electric power at a night game or fans on the field—when neither team is guilty of an infraction or foul. The referee indicates the spot where the drop-ball is to take place and one player from each team prepares to take the drop-ball. The referee then drops the ball between the two designated players, and as soon as it hits the ground play has begun.

THE THROW-IN

As described in Chapter 4, soccer rules are very specific on how a throw-in must be made. The ball must be held with both hands; the ball must be delivered from behind and over the thrower's head; both feet must stay on the ground on or behind the sideline; the thrower, upon re-entering the field of play, can't touch the ball again until it has been touched by at least one other player. Of course, every throw-in provides an excellent opportunity for an offense to get moving. In fact, a quickly taken throw may catch a defense so totally unprepared that a player has a chance for an immediate shoot on goal. Generally, the player making the throw-in is left uncovered by the opposing team. For this reason the ball can almost always be given to a player in a clear space merely by returning it to the thrower. The other players should

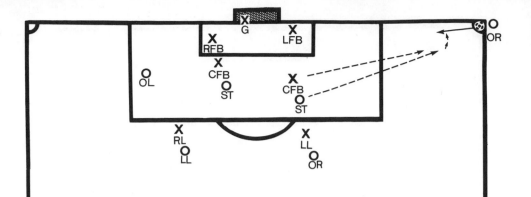

The famous Cosmos sleeper corner kick play, which scores a couple of goals each season. Here's how it works: The striker breaks toward the corner calling for the ball. Then, before reaching the pass spot, he yells "don't," and slows down on his run. Frequently, this will fake the center-fullback and permit the striker to get behind him. If the center-fullback falls for the trick, the outside right forward makes a short pass to the striker, who then has a clear path to goal.

give him plenty of room to work the ball. Shown here are the three offensive throw-in maneuvers that the Cosmos use most frequently. Incidentally, set plays are usually signaled or indicated by the player who starts them or by the captain. For example, if Player A pulls up one of his socks just before putting the ball in play, it means plan #1 is in effect, while if he strokes his hair, plan #2 is going to be used.

Proper synchronization of the throwing and dodging movements of the potential receivers is most important. One way this can be accomplished is: as soon as the ball goes behind the thrower's head in the backswing, the receivers begin their run to free themselves from the covering defensive players. By the time the thrower comes to release the ball he should be able to spot an open man or men. If the receivers haven't been able to get free, the thrower can check his delivery and try again, or throw the ball for a teammate to pass back to him for the orthodox "setting up" play. The players in the field can usually devise many methods of faking the covering opponent, either by individual feints or by interchanges of position.

When the throw-in takes place near the opponents' goal, one attacker can stand on the goal line. He can't be offside from the throw, and even if the ball isn't given to him he can draw at least one defender

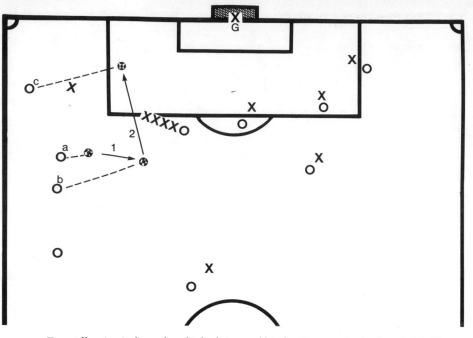

Two offensive indirect free-kick plays used by the Cosmos. In the first *(top),* Player A passes the ball to side. Player B, already in motion, chip-passes the ball. Player C, timing his run, gets possession, and, depending on the situation, he either continues on towards goal or passes the ball to one of the on-running forwards to score. In the second *(bottom),* Player A passes ball to oncoming Player B. He, in turn, makes a "first time" ground pass to Player C, who has timed his break away from the defensive wall. Player C drives the ball into goal. To make this play a success, as Player A approaches the ball, Player D makes a decoy run to take away his opponent, thus creating space for Player B's pass to Player C. Player E makes a decoy run, hoping to draw the defensive wall out of position.

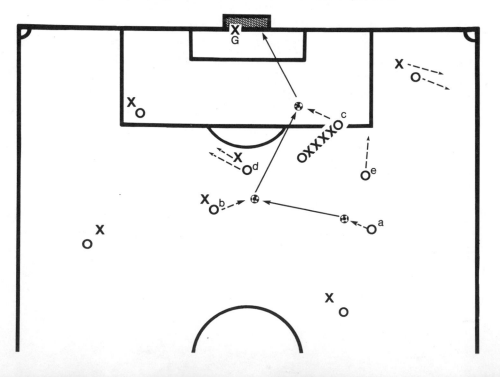

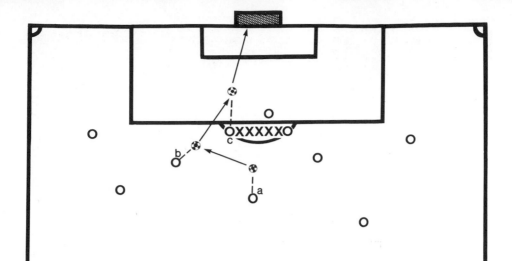

On a free kick against a five-man wall, one of our favorite plays is for **Player A** to pass the ball to Player B, who directs it toward the path of **Player C**. He, in turn, shoots for the goal.

out of position. If the ball is thrown to him, he can head it down for another attacker to shoot directly on goal.

THE CORNER KICK

On the corner kick, the ball can be placed at any point within the quarter circle scribed around the point where the sideline meets the goal line. The diagram here shows the typical positions of attackers and defenders for a corner kick from the right wing. The two fullbacks defend each end of the goal, ready to cover up should the goalkeeper run out to take a high ball. The strikers are covered by the center-fullbacks. Frequently, the outside-left forward is left uncovered because, if the outside-right sends over a high lob to him, the defense will have time to pivot close on him and the right fullback will have time to move off the goal line closer to his man.

The taker of the kick can vary his center. He can send across an "in-swinger," curling in towards the goal, or an "out-swinger," which swerves away. The in-swinger may evade the goalkeeper and will certainly make it difficult for him to catch it as the attack charges in. The out-swinger may tempt the goalkeeper too far out of goal and give the forwards a chance to head or shoot before he can get back. Again, a short ball can be dropped for the inside-right to collect, or a fast low ball can be driven across the goal in the hope that a forward may deflect it. It's very important to practice corner kicks; in an average NASL game we get better than eight. And corner kicks offer one of the best "set" scoring opportunities.

This goal gave the Cosmos the 1972 NASL championship. It was on a penalty kick.

DIRECT AND INDIRECT FREE KICKS

When a referee awards a direct free kick, he places the ball at the spot of the infraction and the offended team has a kick free of any harassment. While a goal can be scored against the offending side as result of such a kick, it's rather difficult since the defenders can form—and almost always do in their half of the field—a wall of players at a point at least 10 yards away from where the ball is being kicked. Unless your team has a banana kicker like our Siggy Stritzl (see page 102), it usually is best to use a free-kick situation to set up and pass into an attacking pattern that will result in a shot at the goal.

The major difference between a direct and indirect free kick is that with the latter a goal can't be scored unless the ball has been played or touched by a player other than the kicker before passing through the goal. Otherwise the play is about the same. As a rule, the play is started by a sure-footed kicker touching the ball a short distance to a teammate who is in position to establish an attack pattern. Frequently we have two of our players converge on the ball as the kicker gets in the free-kick position. The first player will just nudge the ball sideways, and the trailing player will drive the ball on net or to a teammate in scoring position.

THE PENALTY KICK

This is strictly a one-on-one situation—the goalkeeper vs. the shooter. Unlike other sports—this is also true of free kicks—the offended players do *not* necessarily have to take the shot. The coach names the player to take it. On the Cosmos, we usually ask for volunteers. There's a great deal of pressure involved on a penalty kick. Theoretically, with the ball only 12 yards from the goal, the kicker shouldn't ever miss—the average goalie can cover about two-thirds of the goal cage.

Because of vital importance of a penalty kick the Cosmos coaching staff thinks it best to ask for volunteers, and were thankful during our 1972 championship game that Josef Jelinek consented to try the kick if one was forthcoming. With 86 minutes expired, and the score tied 1-1, our linkman Johnny Kerr was fouled in the penalty area. The referee placed the ball at the penalty spot; Josef approached the ball and kicked it. St. Louis Stars' goalie Mike Winter dove for the ball but it caromed off the inside of the left post into the net, giving us a 2-1 decision.

After the game, a reporter asked Josef how he makes a penalty kick. He replied, "I try to keep the ball just off the gound and aim so that the goalie must dive for the ball. It always takes him longer to dive for a ball than to jump up."

If, on a penalty shot, the ball hits the goalkeeper, the crossbar, or the goal posts and bounces back on the field, it is in play and the players, who have kept motionless outside the penalty, must be ready for all eventualities.

THE OFFSIDE TRAP

To beat the offside trap (see page 150) the Cosmos employ three principal methods of attack which can be used in a variety of ways. One is for the player in possession of the ball to break the defense line by dribbling and taking the ball through himself. He can then shoot or turn the ball back to a team member.

Another way to beat the offside trap is to make a square pass—or even a back-pass—to a player who is positioned to run through a space. As shown above, the left striker moves to the left to draw the center-

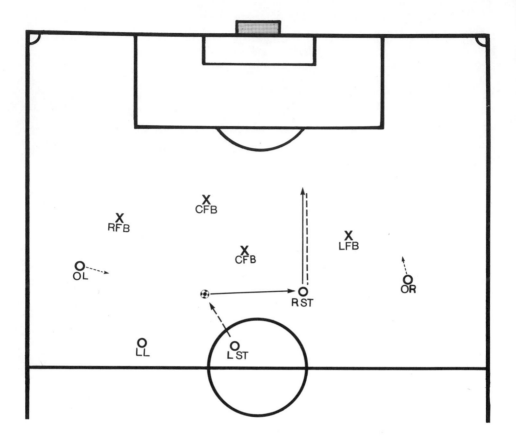

fullback and then passes the ball squarely to the right striker, who is running up to take it through the space between the center-fullback and the left-fullback. Incidentally, when properly performed, the square pass can be an excellent means of beating defenders; but it becomes negative when players, looking for the easy pass, use it as a first choice continually.

A third method is to pass the ball into an open space behind the defensive line for a teammate to run in and reach the ball before the opponents can retrieve it. The pass is delayed to give him time to gain speed, and is made just before he gets into an offside position. If the pass is accurately timed and placed, and if the attacker is a fast runner, he should reach the ball well ahead of the defenders who have to turn before they can start to chase.

Teams should practice methods of beating the "offside" game. To do so, the attackers must learn how to cooperate with each other, conscious all the time that they must avoid offside movements.

A Team on Defense

It has often been said that attack is the best form of defense. While we don't fully subscribe to this statement, there *is* a great deal to say for it. The New York Cosmos is, basically, an offense-minded team, frequently accused by some so-called "experts" and sports writers of abandoning defense at times. But we certainly know and follow the premise that the best way of ensuring a team's continuous attack is to bring effective defensive play into action the moment the ball is lost to the opponents.

As mentioned in Chapter 6, there are two basic methods of defense in soccer (and, for that matter, in most games, such as football, hockey, and basketball): man-for-man and zone defense. The former coverage is self-explanatory: each defender has the specific task of covering one player. As soon as the opposing side obtains possession of the ball, the defender guards his man wherever he moves, either to prevent the ball reaching him or to tackle him should he receive it. The zone, or space, defense provides a player with a roughly defined zone, or area, which it is his responsibility to cover when defending. Any player coming into that zone in possession of the ball becomes his responsibility.

While in amateur soccer circles there's a great deal of controversy as to what method is best, most professional teams use a combination of the two. Few experts disagree that man-for-man coverage gives the most satisfactory type of initial defense. In effect, it is geared to cover every man in the opposing attack, wherever the attack begins to build itself. It tries to maintain at least an equal ratio of defenders to attackers at every stage of the attacking movement. This is especially important when an opponent has skilled players who can exploit immediately any numerical weakness. Whenever an attack begins, the defense should

153

quickly take up position, covering man-for-man, particularly those near the ball through whom an attack will immediately come. Remember that the responsibility for defending or attacking belongs to each player in a team as the situation in play requires it. It should be said here that a man is being covered tightly when an opponent is within immediate challenging distance. The higher the league classification of soccer, the shorter this distance will be, since good players can take advantage of the smallest amount of freedom.

But what happens when an attacker gets past his first covering player? If his continued approach is to be blocked, another defender must leave his man in order to tackle him. Then, of course, the entire balance of man-for-man coverage is upset. Here the principle of zone defense comes into play. Actually, preparation for this change takes place concurrently with man-for-man coverage. That is, close coverage is kept in the area around the ball, but away from this area the defenders relinquish it to follow the zone approach. Should the ball move to another area by a long pass, the defenders near that spot close in to stop the attack while the others move across to give zone coverage. When near the goal, close coverage must be given to every player within shooting range.

Many soccer coaches advise that it is best to start young players off on the principles of zone defense rather than those of man-for-man coverage. The young player, they say, will better appreciate his positional function in a system of zone defense than if he is detailed to shadow one opponent all over the field. Gradually he'll find that his attention is necessarily focused on one player, and will become aware of the need to keep a watchful eye on this opponent. But it's important to keep in mind that a zone defense ignores two important factors. The first is that a team should always try to contain play in the opposing half of the field for as long as possible. Secondly, a player who is in possession of the ball, as well as the players who are within effective range, shouldn't be given complete freedom in which to build up their attacking formations.

DEFENSIVE ORGANIZATION

From the analysis of the need for mobility in attack (see Chapter 7) it's apparent that defensive play is concerned with the maintenance of good coverage at all times. If the movement of attacking players is planned to draw defenders out of position in order to free other attackers, and also to create attacking space, then the defense must be to

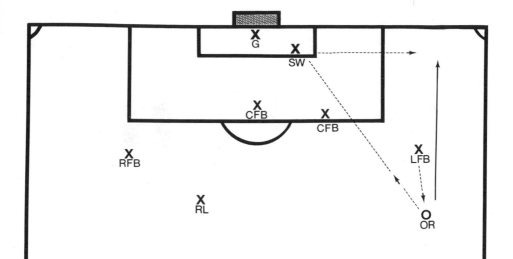

The use of a sweeper has certain advantages. As shown here, the sweeper is the key man in stopping the opposing outside-right forward.

counteract these threats. And, since it's the aim of attacking tactics to get through, around, or over the defensive players it must be the purpose of the defensive organization to stop this aim from becoming a reality.

To obtain a good defensive organization the defenders must position themselves to give complete coverage to their teammates should the attack succeed in breaking through the first stage of man-for-man coverage. Suppose, for instance, in a four-two-four formation one of the center-backs may have to leave the striker he is covering to help out on a breakthrough on the right. The left-fullback must also leave his close coverage of the outside-right forward to be ready to challenge should the attack penetrate successfully. It may be argued that this leaves the outside-right forward free and in an open space, but while the ball is being passed across to him the defenders should have sufficient time to regroup. By the same token, the right-fullback will leave his man to be ready to cover the threat to the center if an attack develops on the other wing. If an attack approaches through the middle, both the right- and left-fullbacks will move in to cover the two strikers. Were the fullbacks to give continuous close coverage on the outside men, the latter would act as decoys to let the strikers penetrate down the middle.

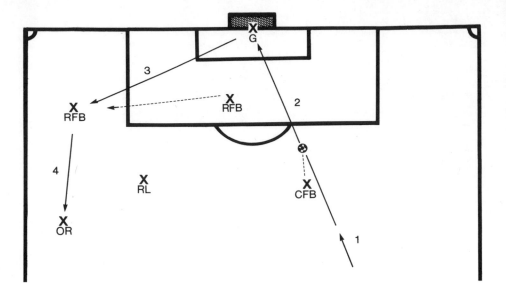

Frequently the goalkeeper can be used as the player to start an offensive play. As shown here, the center-fullback passes back to the goalie, who in turn passes to his right-fullback. He, in turn, passes to his outside-right forward and the attack is underway.

It's not uncommon for attackers to be tightly covered by defenders, particularly when a side's tactical plan is based upon the stopping one "superstar"-type attacking player. When such a player usually finds himself subjected to tight coverage throughout the game he knows in advance that his access to the ball will be severely curtailed. He, then, attempts to draw the opposing defenders into positions where they will be most ineffective. Let's suppose an outside forward is receiving very close coverage from an opposing fullback. If he merely moves into other forward positions he'll be followed by the fullback and the rest of the defenders will cover accordingly. This could create valuable attacking space.

DEFENSIVE TACTICS

Because penetration is a major objective in attack, delay must obviously be the basis of defense. This results from a clear understanding of the order of priorities for a team which has lost possession of the ball. The first consideration, defensively, is the goal, and this will affect play in every portion of the soccer field. Secondly, having lost the ball, a team must be more conscious of the space between defending players and, even more important, behind them. Thirdly, the nearer the attacking side approaches the opposing goal the more closely they must be covered.

Good defensive play necessitates a great awareness of risk. Players on the defensive, and this means the whole of a team when possession has been lost, must pay close attention to their tasks relative to all their teammates. For instance, if an outside forward loses possession of the ball to an opposing fullback in a spot close to the fullback's own goal line, a wild challenge which permits the fullback to beat him is bad defensive play on the forward's part: the challenge may have been spectacular but the mere fact that the fullback beats the forward is enough to expose other members of the defending side to unnecessary problems.

Soccer frequently is a test of patience. A defender should restrain himself so that when he makes a challenge he either stands a *very* good chance of obtaining the ball himself or provides opportunity for one of the other defenders to get it. On attack, a team tests the patience of the defending side by tempting defenders to make poorly calculated challenges and runs. It's safe to say that the closer play comes towards the penalty area the greater the degree of restraint and control that must be exercised by defending players.

There are a few simple examples of lack of restraint in defensive play which typify the problems involved. One is the player who is always drawn towards the ball. Such a "ball-chaser" can easily be tricked into bad or dangerous situations in which attacking space is created between and behind defensive positions.

Another situation influencing the stability of one's defense is the extent to which the players watch the ball. In all defense tactics the restriction of space is of major importance—particularly, as previously stated, space between and behind defensive players. The big danger in watching the ball rather than your man, especially when the ball is not within playing range, is that one or more of the opposing attackers can move into your "blindside" and into spaces behind you. In other words, a natural consequence of ball watching is that you forget your defensive responsibilities and tend to react to the movement of the ball.

Let's see how different types of defensive tactics can be applied at different portions of the field.

DEFENSE IN ATTACKING AREA

Let's suppose our attack has broken down in our opponent's penalty area and their goalkeeper has the ball. Obviously, our team's tactics must be to regain possession, if possible, in that attacking area. At the very least we must try to make accurate and controlled use of the ball very difficult for the opposition. Our attackers will cover the nearest opposing defenders tightly. Their players in midfield will be covered but not so tightly, since the further they are away from goal the greater the time available for our players to move and to challenge. If their team now establishes control of the situation, our attackers will continue to harry them when the ball is near but, at the same time, these players will be increasingly conscious of threatening through-passes in the center of the field. Our midfield players will think principally of retreating in order to make through-passes difficult.

As the opposing attack moves towards the defending area all of the players immediately concerned with defense will fall back to their defensive zones. Reduced to its simplest forms, defense involves:

1. Reducing space.
2. Covering opposing players on a man-for-man basis.

The defensive tactics which we have just studied involve fairly tight man-for-man coverage near the opponent's goal and is known as "a half-field press." Our aim is to regain possession in our opponents' half of the field and to make it difficult for opposing players to keep possession.

SLOW RETREATING DEFENSE

In employing this defense technique, the forwards harass our opponents who are near to them—particularly from behind. They also will always threaten the line of any pass intended to move the ball towards an advanced and central attacking player on the opposing side. They'll try to force opponents in possession of the ball to play square or across the field. Midfield players will tighten up their covering of midfield attackers, while the rearmost defenders will adopt covering positions against possible through-passes.

A team which falls back in front of an opposing side almost inevitably slows it down. In this way the attack is delayed and time for defensive organization is made. Whenever a defender finds that he can't give sufficient cover, it's good practice to make a slow retreat to give his teammates time to run back into position. For example, our

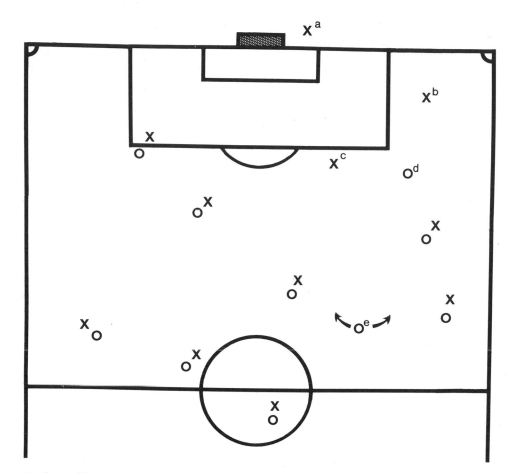

On the goal kick, Player E is the man to watch out for, since he is free. The goalie's (Player A) best play is to either B or C; but in this case Player D could be dangerous.

right-fullback is faced by two attackers. If he tackles the outside-left forward, he'll pass to the one of the strikers who will be able to move into shooting range unopposed. Instead, he positions himself to cover both attackers and retreats slowly. In most cases this will give another player, in this instance the right linkman, time to come back to cover the striker. In soccer, it's most important to keep this thought in mind: *When not in possession, get in position.*

How far and how fast to retreat in this type of defensive tactic depends on many factors. Of course, when their attackers are approaching within shooting range, it becomes necessary to tackle or try to intercept without hesitation. In any case, as the defense nears its own penalty area, its ranks should close. The goalkeeper should be, as an additional defender, ready to come out of goal to gather up any through-pass.

A QUICK RETREATING DEFENSE

In this method of defense, as soon as the opposition gain possession of the ball the entire team drops back in front of the opposing players to produce a series of defensive barriers. The forward barrier threatens the line of through-passes. The more compact the defense, the better the chance of intercepting passes; the more widely spread is the defense, the greater is the opportunity for the attack to exploit the open spaces. Suppose that the linkmen go too far in attack and leave a large gap between them and the rest of the defense. If the opponents get the ball into this space, the linkmen won't be able to recover fast enough, and the defensive backs won't be able to tackle without real danger of having their line broken.

If the linkmen play in close support of the defensive backs, and one of the midfield players is by-passed, the fullbacks can then position themselves to delay the next move while the midfield player recovers. The six defenders should therefore play as a combined unit, unless they intend to take risks deliberately to give more thrust to the attack. Remember that a defender should always be on the goal side of his opposite attacker. If he is on the wrong side of the forward, he could be out of the play all together.

In some quick retreating defense systems, the defenders retreat almost automatically until they reach the penalty area. There they set up a barrier on this narrow front. They don't tackle in midfield and run the risk of early penetration. Instead, they retreat steadily, delaying as they go, and form a strong, compact defense near goal. Territorially, the position seems favorable to the opposing attack, which is approaching seemingly unopposed. In effect, the "barrier" is very difficult to cross. Moreover, if the opposing linkmen are drawn into the attack and the ball is retrieved, the defense can transfer the ball rapidly to its own forwards to start an attacking movement in the big open area in midfield.

DEFENSE AROUND THE GOAL

From the delaying tactics and the defensive priorities which have been established, it should be quite obvious that the final stage of defense is that within and around the penalty area. Equally obviously, the area which offers the greatest opportunity for scoring shots is the central part of this penalty area.

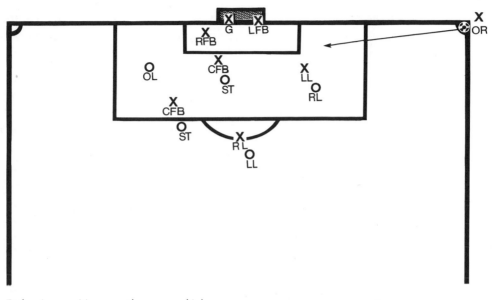

Defensive positions on the corner kick.

Without being too rigid, a reasonable guide to defense can be established as follows: for most players all shots from 20 to 25 yards or less present a scoring threat to the defending side. It may also be said that the finer the angle of the shot, the less likely it is to score. Two imaginary lines projecting outwards, one from each goal post, at an angle of 45 degrees to the goal line, and approximately 30 to 35 yards in length, enclose the central zone of defense. If the foremost defenders are on the outer edge of this zone, the possibility of shots being taken from less than 30 to 35 yards is greatly reduced; and if defenders are concentrated within this arc we can expect few angled shots to score, since we have narrowed the angle. This is, perhaps, an oversimplification, but it will serve as a rough guide. Just as the goalkeeper's job is governed by angles, so all defenders must take into account the angle of attack.

When free kicks are called against a team, the fullbacks (the defenders) should play in relation to the goalie and make any defensive changes he requests. While most people think the goalkeeper would be in the best position to note what the attackers are actually attempting to accomplish, this is not true. For this reason, one of the other players organizes the defensive wall and signals the players to get them into position to cover as many angles as possible. The diagram here shows the various wall formations we employ against a free kick.

DOUBLE COVERAGE

In sports such as football, basketball, and hockey double coverage, or teaming, means that two defense players cover one star attacking player at all times. In soccer this type of coverage is seldom or ever employed. Even a great superstar such as Pele is *not* given such treatment. Most teams assign a player to keep with him at all times. "When I played against Pele in New York," recalls Gordon Bradley, "I stuck to him like a second coat of skin. At half-time I almost followed him into the Santos dressing room."

Tight, or shadow, coverage, in which the main object is to keep the ball away from the attacking player, is frequently employed against a star performer. Mike Renshaw of the Dallas Tornados and Warren Archibald of the Miami Toros receive this treatment quite often during the NASL season. Fortunately, we don't have to do this when we play Dallas. Our Barry Mahy at left-fullback plays Renshaw at outside-right. The defense-offense battles between these two players is generally worth the price of admission to the game.

The word "double coverage" does, however, come up in soccer. This is a type of defense designed to have an extra man available to cover any immediate break through the defensive line. His function is to "plug up" any gaps which develop in the near vicinity of the ball. This principle can be used to good advantage in the case of a throw-in. The linkmen cover their opposing outside forwards, the strikers take the opposing strikers, and one fullback is left free to challenge any movement which eludes the first cover. In the same way, the fullbacks give rear-guard protection to the goalkeeper whenever he moves out to make a high catch.

Speaking of the goalkeeper, there are times when the defender finds himself chasing the ball towards his own goal. In most circumstances it is a sound plan to play the ball back to the goalkeeper. If a player is being challenged for the ball, he is taking an unnecessary risk by attempting to beat his opponent when the goaltender is in a much better position to receive the ball and clear it to a teammate upfield. Defenders may sometimes find it expedient to head the ball back to the goalkeeper when under strong pressure in and around the penalty area. The pass back to the goalie can be used not only for effective

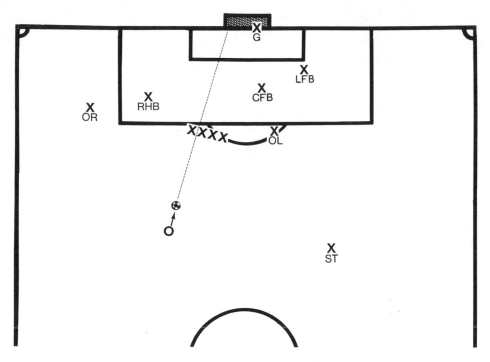

The defensive arrangement of a four-man wall on a free kick.

clearance but also as a quick means of beating the opposing attackers. After making the pass, the defender positions himself for the goal-keeper to return the ball to him immediately—the attacker usually runs on to challenge the goaltender. In short, the defender and the goal-keeper interpass to beat the attacker. Whenever possible, one should play the way he is facing.

Some defenses arrange to pass the ball wide of the goal to make sure that an inaccurate pass won't beat the goalkeeper and enter the net. This seems unnecessarily cautious and, in fact, is as open to error as is any direct pass. No goalie likes to leave his goal wide open by moving to the side, and he may well find himself scrambling to prevent the ball from going over the goal line for a corner. Whatever the case, it is essential to make the pass fast enough to outspeed the attacking for-ward, who will be striving to intercept the ball before it reaches the goalkeeper.

An understanding with the goalie is also necessary in dealing

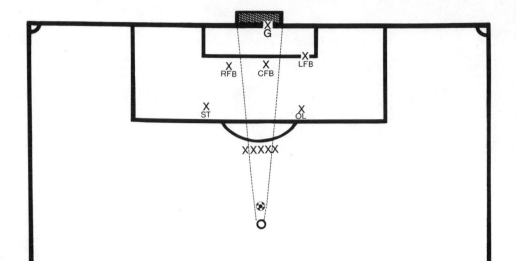

The defensive arrangement of a five-man wall on a free kick.

with high crosses and centers. He can reach much higher with his hands than other players can with their heads, and is best fitted to cut off dangerous lobs in front of goal. But without understanding, the defenders may unwittingly balk him in his advance to catch the ball. When the goalkeeper comes out, the two fullbacks should retreat onto the goal line to protect the goal in case the ball escapes the goaltender. Incidentally, it's wise for the goalkeeper to warn his teammates when he is coming out. But he must not attempt to delude attacking players by this shouting.

OFFSIDE AND THE OFFSIDE TRAP

The offside rule was first introduced to prevent a player from "goal hanging," i.e., lying behind the defenders near the goal in order to score without taking part in the approved action. Actually, before the rule was introduced in 1925, the game frequently was played to groups of players at each end of the field. That is, there were just long passes between a team's defensive and offensive players, and no midfield play at all. But, when the "law" was first introduced, it stated that a player was offside if he was in front of the ball when it was last played and had not at least "three opponents" between him and the opponent's goal line. This rule was quite effective for normal play, but when the defenders began to use the law to nullify genuine attacking movements —sometimes near the half-way line—the game began to lose its attraction. The fullbacks played in front of each other, and the advanced back would run forward to spoil a pass. The rule was altered to state "two players" instead of "three." The change brought about a temporary increase in scoring.

A good forward pass could be made to a player who had moved into a striking position between the backs. Previously, the player had to dribble the ball forward, which gave the backs time to close in. Now, a quick pass allowed attackers to strike before the spread-eagled backs could cover.

Obviously, one defender was needed in front of goal to check all frontal attacks. Hence the "stopper" center-fullback. He blocked the wide gap through the middle. But it wasn't long before *well trained* defenses found that by maintaining a straight line across the field it was still possible to create "offside traps." In some instances, it may prove to be a wise defensive move. For example, if your opponents move downfield toward your goal with four attackers and you and one defender are the only members of your team in position to move back, an offside trap would negate their advantage.

But to be successful an offside trap must be well organized, and the players involved must be able to "read" the intentions of their opponents. Let's say that there is a breakaway down the right side with you (as a center-back, we'll say) and your right-fullback as the only defenders. As their forwards approach and you expect their outside man to pass to a striker, you permit the striker to pass you. As he does this, you signal or call to your fullback to stop. And when he does, the attackers are offside and their fast break is nullified.

As we said, it takes skillful and well trained defenders to plan and work an offside trap. But, keep in mind that when your opponents realize that an offside trap is being formed they'll adopt methods of breaking it (see page 149). These are likely to result in narrow margins of decision as to whether a player is offside or not. If a mistake is made, the path to the goal is wide open.

PLAYING A MAN SHORT

There is only one occasion when a team must play with fewer than eleven players. If a referee sends a player off the field for disciplinary reasons, the player may not return and, unlike any other popular sport, he may *not* be replaced. This is one good reason why it's so important to play fair and to keep one's temper in soccer. Unfortunately, it's usually the player who retaliates against some action of an opposing player that is caught by the referee; the instigator of trouble all too often gets away with the original foul. That happened to our Werner Roth in a recent championship game. He was obviously fouled—obvious to the thousand of spectators, but not seen by the referee—by a St. Louis player, and when Werner retaliated, the Cosmos played the last three minutes with 10 players against 11 opponents.

Fortunately, for us, we were able to hold our 2–1 lead. We say fortunate, since playing a man short in soccer is a most difficult task. Because the field is so large the extra man can raise havoc with a defense. When a player is removed from a game, we try to leave space on the wings. That is, regardless of the position of the player sent off the field, we prefer to leave one of the attacking outside-fullback zones open and cover this player in a zone-type defense.

While the Cosmos play offensive soccer, in a man-short situation we play most defensively. We will, of course, take advantage of all our scoring opportunities, but are happy for a tie in any game when the manpower shortage is against us. When the player advantage is with us, we play a very aggressive offensive game.

While there's no rule against it, we've never heard of a NASL game in which there has been a two-player-short situation. If such a situation should occur, and it could, it would be an almost assured defeat for the short-handed team. Contrary to popular belief, a referee does not have to give a warning to a player before removing him from a game. Because of the burden placed on his team, however, a referee will usually "caution" a player that if he is again considered to be guilty of ungentlemanly conduct he will be ordered off the field.

DEFENSE AND FIELD CONDITIONS

Field and climatic conditions frequently will affect game tactics—both offensively as well as defensively. For instance, players with only average ball control are made to look much better than they are on soft grounds. On hard, bumpy ground, and particularly in strong winds, the same players are in difficulty. The type of pass to be used will also be affected by different playing conditions. On a firm ground, with a wet top, players can increase the range of their ground passes by as much as 25 yards. On very soft ground the range of effective ground passes is reduced considerably, with the added danger of the ball sticking

Artificial turf when wet is like playing on a sponge. Note the water spray as the players run.

half-way to its target. On wet but firm ground, where the slick top surface permits the ball to slide through easily, defenders will definitely have difficulties when they are made to turn. This means that the ball can be passed by the attacking players with a great degree of accuracy and a greater range of passing distance. At the same time the employment of quick, square passing in attack can cause difficulties for the attacking side, since the slightest inaccuracy will cause the receiver to have to turn under difficult conditions. Building-up play should be to the receiver's feet and preferably backward or forward rather than square. In this way the receiver is moving onto the ball and is able to assess the passing possibilities in front of him with the minimum of problems. Defensively, these problem ground conditions will mean that defenders won't be able to commit themselves too readily to tight covering positions or interceptions.

We play all our Cosmo home games, as well as many of our away ones, on Astro-turf. To play on this artificial grass surface requires several adjustments in play. The playing surface is much hotter—about 20 to 30 degrees. The surface is very spongy, especially when wet, and the ball doesn't bounce the same as on regular turf. Sliding tackles, one of the great assets of a good defender, are very difficult to perform on artificial turf.

Under wind conditions, players must support each other more closely in defense to guard against the possibility of the wind causing the ball to do tricks. In attacking play, therefore, considerable use may be made of the low, powerfully driven pass through the opposing defense. A ball so kicked is held by the wind and gives advanced attackers a better opportunity of catching the pass. When playing with the wind remember that the passing range is increased through wind assistance. Crossfield passes are much more effective, but downfield passes have to be carefully determined since they have a tendency to run away from attackers too quickly. The chipped pass is also effective under these conditions, since it is made with a minimum amount of forward movement and the height achieved allows the wind to carry the ball, which results in difficulty for the defenders.

Physical Fitness and Soccer Practice

SKILL is undoubtedly the most important factor in determining either a player's or a team's efficiency in a ball game such as soccer. Even so, a player needs to be fit if he is to develop and express his skill to the highest level of its potential. But neither top-notch physical condition or soccer skills come easily.

To play an entire game, sometimes running as long as 20 minutes without a rest, and still maintain enough stamina for short bursts of speed and booming shots on goal, calls for good overall fitness. All the success achieved by superior skill in a game's early stages can slip away in the last quarter of an hour if a team becomes exhausted and begins to tire.

There are two basic types of soccer conditioning activities: personal and team. Because of our NASL schedule, the Cosmos practice several days a week as a team. However, all our players take part in their own individual circuit training programs. ("Circuit training" is a name given to a series of exercises and routines that alternately stress different systems and muscles of the body.)

PERSONAL FITNESS TRAINING

It's much more interesting to train and practice with your teammates than it is to do fitness activities by yourself, but there is a great deal you can do when practicing alone, if you have to, and, of course, you really concentrate on ways of improving your personal skills and fitness.

Here are some suggestions that you might try in a self-training session. While your activities will depend on the available facilities, you can at least see the framework of a really good workout. When design-

169

A good muscle warm-up exercise: with legs together *(above)* and knees preferably flat on the ground, bounce the ball in front of the feet. Then do the same thing with the legs apart *(right)*.

ing your circuit, be sure to alternate cardiovascular and muscular-skeletal exercises, so that one system recuperates while the other works. For example, when you complete a sprint workout follow it with sit-ups: this allows your cardiovascular system (lungs and heart) to recuperate while your abdominal muscles are taxed.

RUNNING FOR STAMINA AND SPEED

In the average game a soccer player runs from 4 to 7 miles, depending on the position played. Of course running is a basic training exercise in most sports. For as long as we can remember soccer coaches have considered lapping around the field to be an essential fitness routine; in fact, by tradition it has become accepted that six laps is the daily requirement for a soccer player to stay in shape. We disagree with this theory. Lapping the field is the rhythmic type of running and soccer isn't rhythmical. We believe that a soccer player should practice the kind of running into short bursts of walking, jogging, and sprinting. This type of activity is called "interval running" and there are several variations which are suitable to the soccer player's needs.

Interval Running Here's one variation of interval running that many of our Cosmo players use and it is performed as follows:

1. Walk for a distance of 25 yards, jog for 25 yards, and then sprint 25 yards. In the sprint you should always run at your fastest speed. Repeat this exercise several times, then

2. While jogging forward, break into a sprint for 25 yards, suddenly turning around to run backwards for 25 yards. Repeat several times.

3. Jog for about 50 yards and then sprint for a distance of 25 yards; walk, and jog again; then sprint for 50 yards and so on, slowly increasing the distance of the sprint to about 200 yards. It's important that you gradually increase the demand made upon your stamina, until several strenuous circuits of interval running can be done in succession.

Running with the Ball Stamina and running can include skills with the ball. Running practice in which you relate your movement to that of the ball is obviously more in keeping with what you have to do

Any body exercise that incorporates the ball is most helpful in physical conditioning. One of these exercises is shown here: *(top left)* place the ball between the ankles; *(top right)* work the ball up to top of the legs without using hands; *(bottom left)* then work your lower body and allow the ball to roll back down to the ankles; *(bottom right)* repeat the procedure several times.

in a game. Care should be taken, however, to make certain that skills don't absorb so much attention that the purpose of the running is forgotten. Here's a drill that can be most useful.

Run with the ball under control, moving it with the outer portion of the foot. Run at least 200 yards at an easy jog, then do a fast 25 yards, then jog for 25 yards, then a fast 50 yards, then jog 50 yards.

AGILITY AND JUMPING

One can't ignore the fact that the ball is often kicked above head height during a game. Jumping to head or trap the ball are vital skills, and for this reason exercises which will help you to improve your jumping ability and to develop your leg strength should be in your training circuit. For example:

1. Stand with your heels resting on a wedge block or edge of mat, then squat down and return to standing position. Repeat 15 to 20 times.

2. Run over 50 yards, changing length of stride frequently, then include stride leaps, landing with a turn, and roll backwards; get to feet. Repeat over several different distances.

3. Run and hurdle over a series of obstacles about 2 feet 6 inches or 3 feet in height.

4. Power jumping—for instance: run, hop, step, and jump—measuring distance achieved. Attempt to improve distance over a period of training.

5. Jump to head a suspended ball. If possible, the ball should be suspended from a height of 15 to 20 feet. This will give a larger pendulum swing and allow you to head the ball successively. You can jump with both feet together or you can take a few strides and leap with a single foot take-off.

BODY EXERCISES

The list of body exercises is almost inexhaustible, and there are endless variations which can be used to condition a soccer player. Sit-ups, push-ups, trunk-bends, and rope climbing are a few of the more common body exercises that you can use and which can be interspersed into your training circuit along with running and jumping activities. You might try some of the following body exercises which are especially good since they employ a soccer ball:

1. Lie down on your back, holding the ball overhead. Swing the body trunk up to a sitting position, throwing the ball vertically in the air. Throw the ball as high as you can and try to get to your feet to

Practice kicking or tapping the ball lightly in the air. Then bring the action to a stop and try to balance the ball on the instep.

make a catch before it falls to the ground again. Repeat without resting, and try to throw the ball a little further away each time so that you have to scramble quickly to match the catch.

2. Throw the ball high, using a normal throw in action, then run to trap the bouncing ball and bring it back to a given shot. Repeat this, varying the type of trap.

3. Throw the ball high and leap to head it downwards at a wall. Try to flex the trunk and nod vigorously with the head each time. Repeat continuously.

4. Sit on the ball and try to lift both legs to balance in sitting position.

SKILL PRACTICES

Skill practices should be related to your needs or in accordance to your style of play and to the position you play.

Ball Control   To play good soccer, as we have seen, you must possess superior ball-control skills. Here are two simple exercises designed to accustom you to the feel of the ball at your feet:

1. With your feet about 12 to 18 inches apart, stand on your toes and jump lightly from foot to foot. Be sure to raise your feet only a few inches off the ground, also swing the legs from side to side, not forward and backward. After practicing this for several minutes, repeat the motion with a soccer ball between your feet, tapping it smoothly to and from foot to foot. Make certain that the ball remains *on the ground*. Attempt to vary the speed at which you move the ball; that is, change smoothly from a fast to a slow rhythm and back again to fast.

2. Another ball-control exercise is to keep the ball in motion off the ground by kicking or tapping it lightly up in the air in front of you. Start the exercise by allowing the ball to bounce in front of you and learn the trick of flicking a ground ball up in the air with your foot. Flick the ball straight up in the air, and carry on with the exercise. When doing it, employ the area on top of your foot where the instep ends and toes begin to strike the ball, which you should try to keep going up and down between waist and knee height, approximately 12 to 14 inches in front of you. Change the speed of your motion, first bouncing the ball slowly, then increasing the rhythm by tapping the ball higher up to waist level. Practice with both feet.

Here's an exercise that will keep you in shape: *(top left)* kick the ball over the head; *(top right)* do a backward roll; *(bottom left)* then chase the ball; *(bottom right)* and finally bring the ball under control.

Passing   You may be able to kick a ball hard and run fast with it at your toes, but unless you can send a good pass to your teammates, your individual effort may well be wasted, and you can't say that you're a good soccer player. Here are some exercises which deal with a ball coming to you from different directions, and also the distance that you have to push it.

1. Kick the ball against a wall. Start close to the wall and slowly move further away. Keep up a regular rhythm and kick the ball with whichever foot it comes to after bouncing back from the wall. Be sure to turn your hips and shoulder towards the ball as it comes to you so that the inner side of your foot meets it without straining or twisting.

2. As you become more skillful, place a target mark on the wall and however the ball comes to you attempt to hit it back to the target.

3. Stand about a yard away from the wall and try to set up a rhythm of passes at the wall, using each foot alternately.

4. Kick the ball at a wall so that it bounces back at an angle, and then run parallel to the wall to meet it on its return. Kick it back the way it came (try to hit the same spot on the wall), turn around and run back to meet it at the place where you first kicked it. Practice kicking it at different angles and changing the degree of speed.

Shooting   When shooting at the goal you must learn to kick hard and to kick at the ball without having to bring it under control first. It will be difficult at first—you'll miskick more often than not. But after a short time you'll be able to sense the right moment to steady yourself for a shot or to make a pass to someone in a better position for shooting than you are. Here are some good exercises to try against a wall that will help to develop your shot:

1. Kick the ball forward a short way with the inner side of your foot, and then run up to it from a slight angle and try to drive it. Keep practicing until you feel that you are kicking the ball "cleanly" and powerfully each time. Then try to drive the ball at a right angle, either to the left or the right. To do this, kick the ball forward, run after it, and, just before you reach it, turn off slightly —to the *left* if you are going to kick to the *right*. Now come round in a small arc to the right so that when finishing the curve your standing foot will come down beside the ball pointing in the direc-

tion in which the kick is to go. The finish of your turn will help to swing your kicking foot with increased speed and thus a more powerful kick.

2. Throw the ball so that it bounces in front of you. Then step up to it and attempt to kick the ball when it is approximately a foot above the ground. The standing foot should be beside the spot directly underneath the ball at the moment the kick is accomplished. Try not to lean back. Most of the strength for this kick comes from straightening your leg. When approaching the bouncing ball from the side, turn into the kick and lean away from the ball so that your kicking leg gets more swing and therefore more speed. After the kick is completed, turn still a little further on the toes of the standing foot.

3. Throw the ball overhead, then pivot around and make a low volley drive or half-volley drive against a wall. Try this until you can do it smoothly every time.

Heading   It's not always too easy to head a ball, and you will need plenty of practice before you are able to time the ball properly and strike it with your forehead without shutting your eyes. Here are some useful practices:

1. Try to keep the ball airborne by bouncing it off your forehead. Keep the head bent well back and remain on your toes so as to maintain a position directly under the ball. At first, don't attempt to send the ball more than 12 or 18 inches above your head. Then vary the height of the rebound: try to head the ball higher each time. Finish the practice drill by attempting to reduce the rebound and to balance the ball on your forehead. If at any time during the exercise the ball should drop too low to head it, play it with your feet to keep it from touching the ground, then kick it just high enough for you to start the heading drill again.

2. Kick the ball high up against a wall. As it begins to drop to the ground run forward but don't get right underneath it. Instead, position yourself so that the ball will drop just in front of your body. As it is dropping, try to punch at it with your head, tucking your chin well in as you swing your upper body forward. Aim the ball at the bottom of the wall.

3. Try jumping to the ball with the same idea of heading the ball downwards. You'll mistime the ball at first but with practice you will gradually develop the knack of meeting the ball clearly with your

Before a game, players often form heading triangles. Note in this practice that all eyes are on the ball.

forehead at exactly the right moment. Next try heading a ball coming from the side: hit it forward and downward.

Dribbling In the early stages of your development practice dribbling technique by moving the ball along a straight line, varying the speed of the running and the type of dribble. For instance, use alternate feet, or employ only the outside of the foot, or give five pushes with the right foot, followed by five pushes with the left. Also try varying the pace of the dribble. Once you accomplish the basic technique, arrange a line of obstacles about 6 feet apart (sticks, stones—almost anything will do) and weave your way in and out between them with the ball, going to the right of the first obstacle, to the left of the second, and so on down the line. Use both the outside and inside of both feet, keeping the ball completely under close control at all times.

Other Ball-Control Exercises You'll find that you will get into your own way of trapping or controlling a ball that comes to you awkwardly, but try to learn as many ways as you can—particularly those ways which give you the chance to move away quickly with the ball under control. For instance, try throwing or kicking the ball high in the air or against a wall and bringing it gently to the ground by 1) a chest trap, 2) instep, 3) thigh. Also, against a wall, practice continuous volley control, that is, keeping the ball up by playing it with your instep, the upper part of your thigh, your chest and head.

Goalkeeper's Skill Practices   Most goalkeeper's skill practices require another player. Of course, any drills that help you in catching, bouncing, and throwing a ball are good. Here are two good practices that you can perform by yourself:

1. Standing approximately 5 yards from a wall, throw the ball onto the ground so that it then caroms off the wall at different angles. Practice catching the rebounds.
2. Kick the ball at the wall and dive to catch the rebound.

TEAM PRACTICE

Team practices are usually controlled by the coach and each coach has his own favorite drills. Here are a few that we employ during our practice session and try-out camp. Most of the skill drills are performed in a small area—from 10 to 20 yards, depending on the drill.

One on one (Area approximately 10 yards square). Attempt to retain the ball by dribbling your opponent. If your opponent gets possession then he dribbles. Do not go outside designated area.

Two-Against-One Drill (Area: 10 yards).   A two-against-one situation is one of the simplest and best examples of teamwork. It gives an attacking player the opportunity either to dribble past the defender or to beat him by exchanging passes with a supporting attacker. The two-against-one situation is a good time to practice wall passing— soccer's version of the give-and-go. (See page 104.) See how many complete passes you can make before an interception.

Three-Against-One Drill (Area: 10 yards).   The attackers are increased to three but there is still only a single defender. As the man in the middle, he must attempt to intercept the ball while the others interpass it. The defender doesn't have to control it; just getting a foot to it is enough. When he does so, or when the ball goes out of the practice space, the player who made the error becomes the defender.

Two-Against-Two Drill (Area: 10 yards square).   In two-against-two drills, the positions of defenders and attackers are constantly changing as possession is either won or lost by the two teammates.

A two-against-two scrimmage in a small area is very good practice for short passes, controls, positioning, covering, and conditioning. As shown here, we frequently use it to teach ball control to young players.

In these useful practices, gradually increase the numbers of players performing, e.g. 3 on 2, 4 on 3, 5 on 4, until eventually it becomes 11 on 11. When this stage is reached, a great deal of progress should have been made, therefore a better game should be seen. Learning to adapt instantly from defensive to offensive thinking and positioning, and vice-versa, is, as we have stated several times, one of the most important skills of soccer.

Uneven Teams (Area: 30 to 40 yards square). One team has 2 or 3 more players than the other—7 against 4, 9 against 7—so that the larger team has plenty of chance for its players to pass to their teammates. The team with the ball (the larger team) tries to interpass, the other tries to intercept the ball. Passes should vary in length. Players should learn to spread out and take up good positions to make it easy for the one who has the ball to make a good pass.

Dribbling Game (Area: roughly the size of the penalty area). In this five-a-side soccer (confined to dribbling), one team kicks off from the end lines as for a goal kick. After the kick-off, no forward pass is allowed. Players must make ground by dribbling or passing backwards for another player to run forward with the ball. A goal is scored when a player with the ball runs it over the end line and touches it with his foot on the other side. The sides change ends on scoring, and the game is restarted by a goal kick. Throw-ins are taken in the normal way.

There are many other situational games that can be played to make a practice session both interesting and constructive. A good coach will always vary his pratices.

Goalkeeper Practice   The skill of taking a high speed ball safely needs a lot of practice before the goalkeeper can be sure about timing and safe handling. Here are some ways in which you can practice:

1. A player throws the ball with one hand, overhead; the goal-keeper catches it with upstretched arms, at the limit of a jump.

2. This time the goalie stands in position in goal and when he runs out to catch the ball from a long kick, he quickly hugs it to his chest.

3. The high balls to the goalkeeper should be varied so that sometimes the ball drops near the crossbar. In this case, the goal-keeper will use his hand or hands to push or turn the ball over the bar.

4. The ball can be flighted from different areas of the field into the goalmouth. The goalkeeper practices leaving his goal line to catch the ball while being challenged by an opponent.(*Note:* For the first few tries the opponent can act passively but makes the goalkeep-er realize that he is around,) Later the opponent does try to get the ball before the goalkeeper.This then creates a match situation.

It is imperative that the goalkeeper should have a good understand-ing with the defenders so that they know when to take the ball them-selves and when to drop back to cover the goal and leave the high ball to him.

As you practice these methods, you'll gradually get to know just when you can safely leave your goal and when you should stay where you are. There are no rules—it is a matter of judgment, and that will come with experience.

WARM-UP PRACTICE BEFORE A GAME

There are all kinds of "warming-up" activities which can be suitably used to prepare for a game. But for young players it is well worth while using a pre-game session to improve one's skill as well as to warm up and loosen the muscles ready to go all out from the moment of kick-off. Here's a suggested outline of a warming-up session for a team. Instead of standing around in the dressing room or aimlessly kicking in goal with one ball you'll find it much better to build up a routine of practice such as we do with the Cosmos. As you can see, this session emphasizes passing, shooting by forwards, and making clearances by defense, but you can easily substitute other group activities which are designed to meet the specific needs of your team. Note that only half of the field is employed so that the other team can also practice.

PART I (Approximately 10 minutes)

Group 1. The strikers at the goalkeeper—varying their position, distance from goal and type of shot—they also practice fast dribbles at goalkeeper from different angles. Goalie practices handling the ball and running out to take the ball from the center-striker. He also practices accurate throwing.

Groups 2 and 3. The outside men and linkmen practice inter-passing movements approaching goal, using low passes, chipped and volley passes. They also practice throw-in moves.

Group 4. The fullbacks—center, right, and left—practice long low drives, and lob and volley clearances, each taking a turn to work from his defensive in the field. They also practice heading for clearance.

PART II (Approximately 5 minutes)

Group 1. Strikers practice varying interpassing drills and approach plays towards the goal.

Group 2. The defense practices with the goalkeeper, making clearances from long lobs. They must try to build up understanding as to which player should "take" the ball as it comes over towards the goal area. The outside-left and right practice making centers of varying heights, placement, and speeds. They receive service from the linkmen who field the clearances from the "opposing" defense.

PART III (Approximately 5 minutes)

This is a round of purposeful shooting by the forward line. The goalkeeper in this case acts as a fielder, otherwise he is likely to be "peppered" by two or three shots at the same time. The fullbacks also act as fielders behind the goal.

The linkmen act as servers varying the type of ball service to the forwards. The forwards, of course, practice making a variety of shots.

HOW MUCH PRACTICE?

In answer to this question you should first of all ask yourself "How good a soccer player do I wish to become?" To be fit and to become really first class in performance with the ball, you should train and practice hard with the team or by yourself almost every day. But remember that it is what you put into your practice that counts. If your shooting is to become strong you must try to shoot harder every time you go to kick at the goal or a wall. If you want the speed you must drive yourself to move quickly to the ball. Whatever you set your mind to do, keep at it until you achieve some real improvement—and only then go on to other skills. Perfect timing in all aspects of the game is so important.

10

Soccer and the American Player

SOCCER is the sport of the Now generation. The most popular sport in the world has finally caught on in the United States. The present soccer boom in our schools and colleges is remarkable. Statistics show that more than 5,000 high schools are now playing the game. Five years ago there were less than half that number. The increase on the college level is equally impressive. Almost 400 out of over 700 soccer-playing colleges were eligible to participate in the 1972 National Collegiate Athletic Association (NCAA) tournament.

The rise in soccer's popularity comes at a most opportune moment in our history. This is the era of the new individualism in American youth. Soccer fits the bill. As we have seen in this book, it is relevant from the word Go. Relevant because it is dynamic, with non-stop action; because it is a sport for everyone, since size makes little or no difference; because it takes courage and will power; and because it frowns upon conformity. Though it is a team game, it offers opportunity for the true expression of individuality. The player with the ball is the quarterback, using skill and improvisation to maneuver his team toward the goal. The only limits are those imposed by the player's own mind and body.

Before looking at the soccer scene in America, let's take a glance at the world picture. As stated in Chapter 1, the world-wide governing body of soccer is the Fédération Internationale de Football Association, commonly called "FIFA." One of the major responsibilities of FIFA, which is headquartered in Zurich, Switzerland, is to control soccer by taking steps to prevent infringements of the statutes, regulations, and standing orders of the Congress of the FIFA or of the Laws of the Game as laid down by the International Football Association

Preparing to deal with this dangerous dropping ball is Mike Winter, an outstanding American-born player of the NASL. The St. Louis Stars' goalkeeper was the "rookie of the year" in 1972 at seventeen.

Board. It is through FIFA that individual countries are sanctioned.

The major international event is, of course, for the Jules Rimet Trophy, commonly called the World Cup. This competition takes place in a different country every four years and was first held in 1930. This is a contest for national all-star teams, not national club champions. That is, each country that belongs to the FIFA selects the best players from each of that country's teams, who then train together as a unit. These all-star teams then play regional eliminating rounds.

The FIFA is divided into six continental confederations: Europe, Asia, Africa, South America, Oceania (Australia, New Zealand, and the Pacific Islands), and Concacaf (Carribean Islands, North America, and Central America). The United States thus takes part in the Concacaf regional qualifications.

The winners, plus some of the better teams in the regional qualifications—16 in all—play in the World Cup finals. Winning countries of the World Cup to date are: 1930, Uruguay; 1934, Italy; 1938, Italy;

1950, Uruguary; 1954, West Germany; 1958, Brazil; 1962, Brazil; 1966, England; 1970, Brazil. The next World will be held in West Germany in 1974.

Another important international all-star soccer competition is the Olympic Games. While the World Cup is open to both amateur and professional players, the Olympic team must be completely amateur.

In addition to the international all-star team competitions, there are regional internationals for national club champion teams. The two major ones are the European Cup and Copa Libertadores contested by national club champions of each European and South American country respectively. In the last few years, the African, Asian, and Concacaf Cups have increased in stature in world soccer circles. There are many other lesser international competitions, and in any given week there are bound to be at least a dozen major professional soccer teams traveling somewhere in the world to another country for some kind of competition.

Although the United States Soccer Football Association has been a member of FIFA since 1913, only a few events worthy of international recognition have been recorded. Our most remarkable success, of course, was the 1-0 victory over England during the 1950 World Cup competition. This victory, and a 1966 win by little North Korea over the giants of Italy, rank as the most startling upsets on the international sporting front. The ethnic backgrounds of the 1950 United States winners included Belgium, England, Italy, Ireland, Scotland, Portugal, and the United States, with Haitian-born center-forward Joe Gaetjens scoring the game's only goal.

We came in contact with unsung hero Gaetjens—or at least his family—in the saddest of circumstances in 1971. His two brothers, Jean and Gerard, came to tell us that no one had heard from, or of, Joe since he had been arrested in Haiti by the secret police of now-dead dictator "Papa Doc" Duvalier in 1964. His wife Lilian and their three sons did not know if Joe was still alive in prison or if he had been executed. We helped form the Joe Gaetjens Foundation and enlisted the aid of many of the superstars in that beaten English team—not to mention Joe's old teammates like Walter Bahr of Philadelphia, whose son, Ensign Casey Bahr, was to be one of the 1972 U.S. Olympic stars. But to no avail. We believe, as does his family, that Joe Gaetjens, scorer of one of the most stunning goals in history, is dead, executed in the regime of a maniac—but we can't be sure.

The other United States achievements in soccer worth mentioning

Siggy Stritzl (Number 15, above) is an outstanding product of New York City's high schools and an All-City in 1961, when he helped lead Grover Cleveland High School to the PSAL title. In addition to playing professional soccer, Siggy played

have to be traced back to the 1930's: there were two 3-0 victories over Belgium and Paraguay in the World Cup competition in 1930 at Montevideo, and the participation of the United States team in the World Cup in 1934 in Italy.

In view of the fact that soccer has been popular the world over for generations, it seems strange that the many waves of immigrants have failed to carry this enthusiasm along with their other cultural modalities. Perhaps it's a matter of image: the game in other countries has been traditionally a game for the poor; it was a poor man's recreation, with an "other-side-of-the-tracks" stigma. The newcomer to America doesn't want to identify with such negativism. Perhaps he unconsciously feels he must renounce it and look for a more positive image in his new life. The immigrant didn't realize that the sport is greatly admired here, that involvement is an immediate means of communication, and that Americans have had a long tradition of encouraging sport participation in their schools and colleges.

To those who argue that soccer is most popular in densely populated "foreign" areas, we'd like to point out that this isn't necessarily a benefit. More often than not it is due to the failure of these particular "foreign" groups to absorb the new culture or to allow any part of their

for the United States World Cup and Olympic teams. American-born Stan Startzell (Number 14, above) was an All-American college soccer player and was drafted Number Two by the Cosmos in the 1972 NASL draft.

own culture to be taken from them. They carry on the game, as they did at home, in minority cliques, and with no receptiveness to either American influence or American participation. As a result, their influence on the game has been, until recently, minimal.

But it is in the blending of new American-born players with talented pros from abroad that the future of American soccer lies. The mixture will someday produce the long-awaited soccer superstars, similar to the superstars who have done so much to put other sports on the map. America's Pele—or soccer's Joe Namath—is alive and playing somewhere on the soccer fields of Long Island or Seattle—or someplace in between.

If we are going to have good American players we must develop them in our grassroots. Granted, some have the opportunity to play at the college level and that a select few are chosen to represent the United States in international competition whenever an Olympic, Pan American, or World Cup competition comes around. But this is only a drop in the ocean.

Until recently very few Americans could make a professional or national team. To be perfectly candid, very few collegians can be termed "natural" soccer players. They are lacking in the basic skills of

Our future "superstars" have to remember to keep their eyes open.

the game, because of the lack of experience, competition, and opportunity in their early days of playing. Such weaknesses *can* be partially overcome, especially by young men whose intellects are alive and susceptible to coaching and the desire for improvement. What college students may lack in the general skills of the game at this stage can be largely countered by assets such as teamwork and a persistent resolution to succeed. The American players may be less sophisticated than their foreign counterparts, but they will mature with experience. And the younger they are, the better players they will be. We can hardly wait for them to grow up.

We must have a clear-cut, streamlined program from the school to the club and professional levels, with frequent international competition. This will overcome the past stagnation in the game and automatically lead to a representative national team. We in the Cosmos organization have long believed that instead of club and pro teams nurturing little foreign cliques, they should open their doors to American players who have a natural determination and a zest for playing. You cannot

Boys from the age of seven to fourteen play before and during half-time at all Cosmos home games. Wonderful enthusiasm is shown by both players and fans to these youth games.

expect our college players and coaches to wax enthusiastic over a domestic game that is dominated by other nationalities, where even communication is hardly possible. Teams should be required to use American players. For example, other nation's regulations may limit a club or pro roster to no more than three or four foreign players. This is not uncommon. It is observed by nations who realize it is suicidal to choke off opportunity for the home-bred players.

The USSFA, with full cooperation of NASL, in 1969, set up a committee to formulate ways and means of administering a national youth soccer league. The principal aim of such a program would be to bring together and give a common sense of purpose to the myriad young groups now playing soccer and to encourage the formation of new teams and leagues for boys ages seven through fifteen who will eventually participate in the sport at the national level. The number of youth teams in the entire country is colossal.

In a city like Seattle, for example, more than eight hundred youth teams have been set up in less than eight years. They are practicing and

Coach Gordon Bradley gives "the word" to young soccer players at the Cosmos Soccer Academy.

playing regularly, but they do not belong to senior clubs. There has been an exchange program in existence for years between Vancouver, Canada and Seattle, Washington in which six hundred youth teams from both sides are participating. On a long weekend six hundred Seattle youth teams go by bus or private car to Vancouver to play there, and six hundred Vancouver teams come to Seattle for the return matches. Nowhere in the world is there any comparable program.

The basic philosophy underlying all youth competition is that every boy shall be given the opportunity to play, although the number of practices and number of games played is left up to individual local leagues. It is highly recommended that practices be restricted to a maximum of two sessions weekly for a maximum of one and one-half hours and that one league game be played weekly. It is also imperative that a boy who attends practices regularly must be allowed to play at least half of every game. No one must be denied the opportunity to play because of lack of ability.

Several of the professional teams and many college and high school coaches run player and coaching clinics for youth groups and other interested organizations. In addition, summer soccer schools and camps are starting up across the country. We operate the Cosmos Soccer Academy for several week-long sessions each summer at our home field —Hofstra Stadium—on Long Island. This school is conducted by Gordon Bradley with the teaching staff made up of the New York Cosmos players.

Soccer football in the United States is a sleeping giant. The impossible will become possible, when someone who knows the aim can also show the way to do it. European experiences may serve as examples but they cannot be transferred to American proportions. United States soccer has to study European football and then to find the American way. The aim is well known; to reach it team spirit and team work of all soccer playing groups in the country are required. We must remember that the organization of soccer in the United States is vastly different than its organization anywhere else in the world.

One of the main reasons is our educational system. In other soccer countries of the world, the number of men who go to college is infinitesimal when compared to the number of people who go to schools of higher learning in the United States. There is, therefore, no college pool of talent nor is there the protectiveness of the NCAA over the college athlete. In Europe, then, many boys are signed to professional contracts as young as ten. For instance, in England a major league club can legally sign, with parental consent, an eleven-year-old boy to an *apprentice* professional contract. In Italy the major league teams obtain their players younger and send them to special soccer schools. Here, Italy's future superstars from all around the country receive their regular school lessons as well as the training to play soccer the professional way.

The great Pele came from a poor village in the interior of Brazil; a friend of his father paid his way to tryout camps. After failing two tryouts, the frail little boy of fourteen was taken by the Santos. That first year he made the first team. When he was only seventeen years old, he scored two goals in the World Cup Final in Stockholm and has absolutely staggered the world since then by being, except on very few occasions, unstoppable. He has scored more goals than any man in the history of the game—somewhere like fourteen hundred. He has drawn capacity crowds in every country he's visited, including the United States and Canada. He has more honors than any middle-European prince who has printed his own. Every country he has gone to has honored him—from welcome from President Nixon to being named honorary President of Guadaloupe. He has ridden with the President of France through crowds of hundreds of thousands along the Champs Elysée. He has dined with kings, been embraced by ambassadors. During the Biafra-Nigerian War, the fighting was stopped for a day so he could cross into Biafra from Nigeria to play an exhibition game. And after he played the exhibition game, the war stopped for another day so that he could be escorted by the two armies back across the border again. He is probably the only truly *international* sports hero that there is or has ever been.

Soccer is about the only sport in which sixteen- to eighteen-year-olds can compete on a professional basis with older players. Could you imagine even an eighteen-year-old playing in the National Football League? The sheer aging adult strength of the players around him would tear him to shreds. But in soccer a sharp, quick, and intelligent athlete of sixteen doesn't have to worry about the lack of sheer brute strength. If a boy is skilled enough, he is often old enough. Our goalkeeper, Richie Blackmore, was only eighteen when we won the NASL championship in 1972, and by then he had already had professional experience in England. Of course, if he were an American, we couldn't, under NCAA rules, help him until after his college class graduated.

In spite of such handicaps, we'll soon have many American-born players in our league. The St. Louis Stars, for instance, had seven St. Louis-born players on the 1972 team which reached the NASL playoff finals. In 1972 the North American Soccer League also had its first college talent draft. Several drafted players, including Philadelphia Textile Institute's Barry Barto, University of Pennsylvania's Stan Startzell, San Francisco University's Otey Cannon, made it with NASL teams.

With the recent developments in American soccer a boy of seven, thanks to the various youth programs and great interest in high schools and colleges, can now look to fourteen years of pleasure in the sport. At the end of this time, he may find himself engaged, as either a professional participant or as a spectator, in a sport that will not only be a domestically popular game, but a game which he may play or see in Moscow, Rio de Janeiro, Buenos Aires, or elsewhere in the world. Soccer is the Now game for the Now generation—of every size, shape, race, color, creed, or sex, in every part of every land in the world.

Glossary
of Soccer Terms

CENTER. To pass the ball from a wide position on the field into the penalty area.

CHARGE. Pushing the opponent off legally by shoulder-to-shoulder contact.

CLEARANCE. A throw or kick by the goalkeeper or a kick by the defender in an attempt to get the ball away from the goal area.

CORNER KICK. The kick awarded to the offensive team at the place where the sidelines and goal lines meet. It occurs when a member of the defensive team plays the ball over his own goal line but not into his goal.

CROSS. See *Center.*

DRAW. The scores of both teams are even; same as a *tie.*

DRIBBLE. A way of advancing the ball past defenders by a series of short taps with one or both feet.

DROP-BALL. A ball dropped into play at the point where play stopped by the referee between two opposing players after a stoppage in the game (such as for an injured player), when a goal has not been scored or a foul committed.

END LINE. See *Goal Line.*

FIFA. Fédération Internationale de Football Association, the world governing body of soccer.

FOUL. Any act contrary to the Laws of the Game.

FOUR-THREE-THREE (4–3–3). A system of play that uses a line of four defenders, three midfield players, and three strikers.

FOUR-TWO-FOUR (4–2–4). A system of play that uses, in front of a goalkeeper, a line of four defenders, two midfield players, and four offensive forwards or strikers.

FREE KICK. A kick awarded when a member of the opposing team commits a foul. The ball is placed on the spot where the foul occurred and a player has a "free kick" at it.

FREE KICK—DIRECT. Awarded for the more serious fouls. May be shot directly into the goal.

FREE KICK—INDIRECT. Awarded for lesser fouls. Must be touched by the kicker and at least one other player before a goal can be scored.

GOAL AREA. The zone, 6 yards by 20 yards, inside each penalty area in front of each goal.

GOAL KICK. The kick taken by the goalkeeper to restart play when his opponents have put the ball over the goal line—outside the goal.

GOAL LINE. The line drawn at each end of the field of play. Also called "end lines."

GOAL NETS. The nets draped from the goalposts to stop the ball when a goal has been scored. They must be fixed tightly to the goal posts so that the ball cannot squeeze through.

GOAL POSTS. The two uprights (8 feet high) and one crossbar (8 yards long) that make up the goal at each end of the field.

HALF-VOLLEY. Kicking the ball just as it is rebounding off the ground.

HALF-WAY LINE. The line drawn across the middle of the field to divide it into equal halves.

HANDS. The foul committed when a player, other than the goalkeeper, touches the ball with his hands or arms on the field of play.

HAT TRICK. Three goals scored by one player in succession in the same game.

HEADING. A method of scoring, passing and controlling the ball by making contact with the head.

INTERNATIONAL. The title given to a player who has played for his nation's all-star team against foreign opposition.

KICK-off. The kick from a spot in the center of the field, which starts the game and restarts it at half-time and after each goal.

LINESMEN. The two officials who assist the referee. They remain off the field of play on the sidelines.

LINKMAN. A midfield player.

LOB. A high, soft kick taken on the volley, lifting the ball over the heads of the opponents.

MARKING. Guarding an opponent.

NASL. The North American Soccer League.

OBSTRUCTING. Preventing the opponent from going around a player by standing in his path.

OFFSIDE. Occurs if the ball is passed to a player by a member of his own team, the player being in the opponents' half of the field with fewer than two opponents between him and the opponents' goal when the ball was last played.

OWN GOAL. When a player accidentally puts the ball into his own goal. The score is counted for the other team, and the man who made the mistake is "credited" with scoring an "own goal."

OVERLAP. The attacking play of a defender going down the touchline past his own winger.

PASS. The movement of the ball from one player to another.

PENALTY AREA. The zone, 18 yards by 44 yards, in front of each goal.

PENALTY KICK. A kick at the goal, taken from a point 12 yards from the middle of the goal (penalty spot) when the defending team has committed a major foul inside the penalty area.

PITCH. Another name for the field of play.

REFEREE. The official in sole charge of the game, assisted by two linesmen.

SAVE. The goalkeeper stopping an attempted goal by catching or deflecting the ball away from the goal.

SCREEN. Retaining possession and protecting the ball by keeping your body between the ball and opponent.

SHOT. The kick at the goal made with the aim of scoring a goal.

SIDELINES. See touchlines.

SLIDING TACKLE. Attempting to take the ball away from the opponent by sliding on the ground.

STRIKER. A central forward position in the team with a major responsibility for scoring goals.

SWEEPER. A defender who roams either in front of or behind the fullback line to pick up stray passes.

TACKLING. Attempting to take the ball away from an opponent when both players are playing the ball with their feet.

THROW-IN. When the ball goes over the sidelines and is thrown back into play by a member of the team that did not touch it last.

TOUCHLINES. The lines drawn at each side of the field. Also called sidelines.

TRANSFER FEE. The sum paid by one club to another for a player's contract.

TRAP. Controlling a ball passed close to the player by means of the feet, thighs or chest.

VOLLEY. Kicking the ball while it is in flight.

USSFA. United States Soccer Football Association, the governing body of United States soccer.

WALL PASS. A pass to a teammate followed by a first time return pass, for you to collect on the other side of the opponent (give and go).

WING. An area of the field near the sideline.

WINGER. Name given to the right and left outside forwards.

WING HALF. The player on either flank in midfield who does either offensive or defensive jobs.

WORLD CUP. The championship for national all-star teams. The eliminations take two years, and the finals are played in a different country every four years. The correct name of the trophy was the Jules Rimet Trophy, named after the Frenchman who founded FIFA. Brazil retired the trophy after winning it three times. The new trophy is called the FIFA World Cup.

Appendix

LAW I.—THE FIELD OF PLAY

The Field of Play and appurtenances shall be as shown in the following plan:

(1) **Dimensions.** The field of play shall be rectangular, its length being not more than 130 yards nor less than 100 yards and its breadth not more than 100 yards nor less than 50 yards. (In International Matches the length shall be not more than 120 yards nor less than 110 yards and the breadth not more than 80 yards nor less than 70 yards.) The length shall in all cases exceed the breadth.

(2) **Marking.** The field of play shall be marked with distinctive lines, not more than 5 inches in width, not by a V-shaped rut, in accordance with the plan, the longer boundary lines being called the touch-lines and the shorter the goal-lines. A flag on a post not less than 5 ft. high and having a non-pointed top, shall be placed at each corner; a similar flag-post may be placed opposite the halfway line on each side of the field of play, not less than 1 yard outside the touch-line. A halfway-line shall be marked out across the field of play. The centre of the field of play shall be indicated by a suitable mark and a circle with a 10 yards radius shall be marked round it.

(3) **The Goal-Area.** At each end of the field of play two lines shall be drawn at right-angles to the goal-line, 6 yards from each goal-post. These shall extend into the field of play for a distance of 6 yards and shall be joined by a line drawn parallel with the goal-line. Each of the spaces enclosed by these lines and the goal-line shall be called a goal-area.

(4) **The Penalty-Area.** At each end of the field of play two lines shall be drawn at right-angles to the goal-line, 18 yards from each goal-post. These shall extend into the field of play for a distance of 18 yards and shall be joined by a line drawn parallel with the goal-line. Each of the spaces enclosed by these lines and the goal-line shall be called a penalty-area. A suitable mark shall be made within each penalty-area, 12 yards from the mid-point of the goal-line,

201

measured along an undrawn line at right-angles thereto. These shall be the penalty-kick marks. From each penalty-kick mark an arc of a circle, having a radius of 10 yards, shall be drawn outside the penalty-area.

(5) **The Corner-Area.** From each corner-flag post a quarter circle, having a radius of 1 yard, shall be drawn inside the field of play.

(6) **The Goals.** The goals shall be placed on the centre of each goal-line and shall consist of two upright posts, equidistant from the corner-flags and 8 yards apart (inside measurement), joined by a horizontal cross-bar the lower edge of which shall be 8 ft. from the ground. The width and depth of the goal-posts and the width and depth of the cross-bars shall **not exceed 5 inches (12 cm).** **The goal-posts and the cross-bars shall have the same width.**

Nets may be attached to the posts, cross-bars and ground behind the goals. They should be appropriately supported and be so placed as to allow the goal-keeper ample room. (**Note: Goal nets.** The use of nets made of hemp, jute or nylon is permitted. The nylon strings may, however, not be thinner than those made of hemp or jute.)

LAW II.—THE BALL

The ball shall be spherical; the outer casing shall be of leather or other approved materials. No material shall be used in its construction which might prove dangerous to the players.

The circumference of the ball shall not be more than 28 in. and not less than 27 in. The weight of the ball at the start of the game shall be not more than 16 oz. nor less than 14 oz. The pressure shall be equal to atmospheric pressure (i.e. 15 lb. per sq. in. $= 1 \text{kg/cm}^2$ at sea level). The ball shall not be changed during the game unless authorised by the Referee.

LAW III.—NUMBER OF PLAYERS

[1] A match shall be played by two teams, each consisting of not more than eleven players, one of whom shall be the goalkeeper.

[2] Substitutes, up to a maximum of 2 per team, are permitted in a friendly match and also, provided that the authority of the International Association(s) or National Association(s) concerned has been obtained, in a match played under the rules of a competition. The Referee shall be informed of the names of substitutes (if any) before the start of the match.

[3] One of the other players, or a named substitute (if allowed) may change places with the goalkeeper, provided that notice is given to the Referee before the change is made

Punishment: If, without the Referee being notified, a player or a named

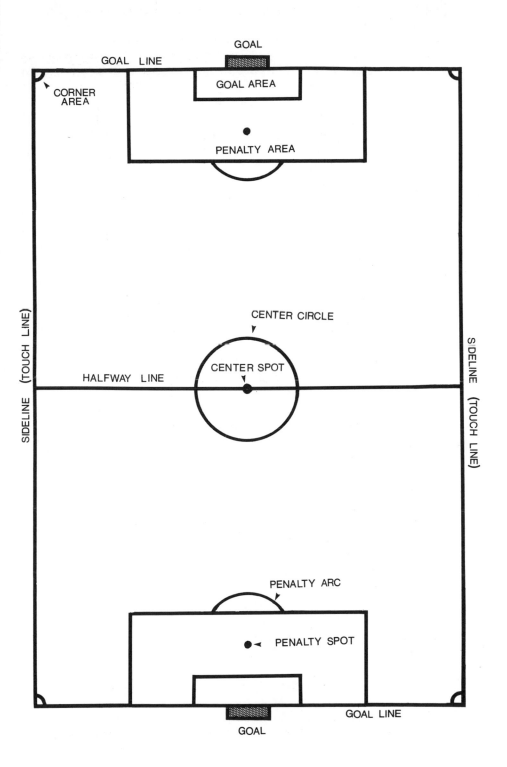

substitute changes places with the goalkeeper during the game, at the half-time interval, or at any other interval in a game in which extra time is played, and then handles the ball within the penalty area, a penalty-kick shall be awarded.

LAW IV.—PLAYERS' EQUIPMENT

A player shall not wear anything which is dangerous to another player. Boots must conform to the following standard:

(a) Bars shall be made of leather or rubber and shall be transverse and flat, not less than half an inch in width and shall extend the total width of the boot and be rounded at the corners.

(b) Studs shall be made of leather, rubber, aluminium, plastic or similar material and shall be solid. With the exception of that part of the stud forming the base, which shall not protrude from the sole, more than one quarter of an inch, studs shall be round in plan and not less than half an inch in diameter. Where studs are tapered, the minimum diameter of any section of the stud must not be less than half an inch. Where metal seating for the screw type is used, this seating must be embedded in the sole of the boot and any attachment screw shall be part of the stud. Other than the metal seating for the screw type of stud, no metal plates even though covered with leather or rubber shall be worn, neither studs which are threaded to allow them to be screwed on to a base screw that is fixed by nails or otherwise to the soles of boots, nor studs which, apart from the base, have any form of protruding edge rim or relief marking, or ornament, should be allowed.

(c) Combined bars and studs may be worn, provided the whole conforms to the general requirements of this law. Neither bars nor studs on the soles or heels shall project more than three-quarters-of-an-inch. If nails are used they shall be driven in flush with the surface.

(N.B.—The usual equipment of a player consists of a jersey or shirt, shorts, stockings and boots. A goalkeeper shall wear colours which distinguish him from the other players.)

Punishment: For any infringement of this Law, the player at fault shall be sent off the field of play to adjust his equipment and he shall not return without first reporting to the Referee, who shall satisfy himself that the player's equipment is in order; the player shall only re-enter the game at a moment when the ball has ceased to be in play.

LAW V.—REFEREES

A Referee shall be appointed to officiate in each game. He shall:

(a) Enforce the Laws and decide any disputed point. His decision on points

of fact connected with the play shall be final so far as the result of the game is concerned. His jurisdiction begins from the time he signals for the kick-off, and his power of penalising shall extend to offences committed when play has been temporarily suspended or when the ball is out of play. He shall, however, refrain from penalising in cases where he is satisfied that by doing so he would be giving an advantage to the offending team.

(b) Keep a record of the game; act as timekeeper and allow the full or agreed time, adding thereto all time lost through accident or other cause.

(c) Have discretionary power to stop the game for any infringement of the Laws and to suspend or terminate the game whenever, by reason of the elements, interference by spectators, or other cause, he deems such stoppage necessary. In such a case he shall submit a detailed report to the competent authority, within the stipulated time, and in accordance with the provisions set up by the National Association under whose jurisdiction the match was played. Reports will be deemed to be made when received in the ordinary course of post.

(d) Have discretionary power, from the time he enters the field of play, to caution any player guilty of misconduct or ungentlemanly behaviour and, if he persists, to suspend him from further participation in the game. In such cases the Referee shall send the name of the offender to the competent authority, within the stipulated time, and in accordance with the provisions set up by the National Association under whose jurisdiction the match was played. Reports will be deemed to be made when received in the ordinary course of post.

(e) Allow no person other than the players and linesmen to enter the field of play without his permission.

(f) Stop the game if, in his opinion, a player has been seriously injured; have the player removed as soon as possible from the field of play, and immediately resume the game. If a player is slightly injured, the game shall not be stopped until the ball has ceased to be in play. A player who is able to go to the touch or goal-line for attention of any kind, shall not be treated on the field of play.

(g) Have discretionary power to suspend from further participation in the game, without previous caution, a player guilty of violent conduct.

(h) Signal for recommencement of the game after all stoppages.

(i) Decide that the ball provided for a match meets with the requirements of Law II.

LAW VI.—LINESMEN

Two Linesmen shall be appointed, whose duty (subject to the decision of the Referee) shall be to indicate when the ball is out of play and which side is entitled to the corner-kick, goal-kick, or throw-in. They shall also assist the Referee to control the game in accordance with the Laws. In the event of undue interference or improper conduct by a Linesman, the Referee shall dispense with his services and arrange for a substitute to be appointed. (The matter shall be reported by the Referee to the competent authority.) The Linesmen should be equipped with flags by the Club on whose ground the match is played.

LAW VII.—DURATION OF THE GAME

The duration of the game shall be two equal periods of 45 minutes, unless otherwise mutually agreed upon, subject to the following: *(a)* Allowance shall be made in either period for all time lost through accident or other cause, the amount of which shall be a matter for the discretion of the Referee; *(b)* Time shall be extended to permit a penalty kick being taken at or after the expiration of the normal period in either half.

At half-time the interval shall not exceed five minutes except by consent of the Referee.

LAW VIII.—THE START OF PLAY

*(a)*At the beginning of the game, choice of ends and the kick-off shall be decided by the toss of a coin. The team winning the toss shall have the option of choice of ends or the kick-off.

The Referee, having given a signal, the game shall be started by a player taking a place-kick (i.e., a kick at the ball while it is stationary on the ground in the centre of the field of play) into his opponents' half of the field of play. Every player shall be in his own half of the field and every player of the team opposing that of the kicker shall remain not less than 10 yards from the ball until it is kicked-off; it shall not be deemed in play until it has travelled the distance of its own circumference. The kicker shall not play the ball a second time until it has been touched or played by another player.

*(b)*After a goal has been scored, the game shall be restarted in like manner by a player of the team losing the goal.

*(c)*After half-time; when restarting after half-time, ends shall be changed and the kick-off shall be taken by a player of the opposite team to that of the player who started the game.

Punishment. For any infringement of this Law, the kick-off shall be retaken except in the case of the kicker playing the ball again before it has been touched or played by another player; for this offence, an indirect free-kick shall be taken by a player of the opposing team from the place where the infringement occurred. A goal shall not be scored direct from a kick-off.

*(d)*After any other temporary suspension; when restarting the game after

a temporary suspension of play from any cause not mentioned elsewhere in these Laws, provided that immediately prior to the suspension the ball has not passed over the touch or goal-lines, the Referee shall drop the ball at the place where it was when play was suspended and it shall be deemed in play when it has touched the ground; if, however, it goes over the touch or goal-lines after it has been dropped by the Referee, but before it is touched by a player, the Referee shall again drop it. A player shall not play the ball until it has touched the ground. If this section of the Law is not complied with the Referee shall again drop the ball.

LAW IX.—BALL IN AND OUT OF PLAY

The ball is out of play:

(a) When it has wholly crossed the goal-line or touch-line, whether on the ground or in the air.

(b) When the game has been stopped by the Referee.

The ball is in play at all other times from the start of the match to the finish including:

(a) If it rebounds from a goal-post, cross-bar or corner-flag post into the field of play.

(b) If it rebounds off either the Referee or Linesmen when they are in the field of play.

(c) In the event of a supposed infringement of the Laws, until a decision is given.

LAW X.—METHOD OF SCORING

Except as otherwise provided by these Laws, a goal is scored when the whole of the ball has passed over the goal-line, between the goal-posts and under the cross-bar, provided it has not been thrown, carried or propelled by hand or arm, by a player of the attacking side, except in the case of a goalkeeper, who is within his own penalty-area.

The team scoring the greater number of goals during a game shall be the winner; if no goals, or an equal number of goals are scored, the game shall be termed a "draw".

LAW XI.—OFF-SIDE

A player is off-side if he is nearer his opponents' goal-line than the ball **at the moment the ball is played unless:**

(a) He is in his own half of the field of play.

(b) There are two of his opponents nearer to their own goal-line than he is.

(c) The ball last touched an opponent or was last played by him.

(d) He receives the ball direct from a goal-kick, a corner-kick, a throw-in, or when it was dropped by the Referee.

Punishment. For an infringement of this Law, an indirect free-kick shall be taken by a player of the opposing team from the place where the infringement occurred.

A player in an off-side position shall not be penalised unless, in the opinion of the Referee, he is interfering with the play or with an opponent, or is seeking to gain an advantage by being in an off-side position.

LAW XII.—FOULS AND MISCONDUCT

A player who intentionally commits any of the following nine offences:

(a) Kicks or attempts to kick an opponent;

(b) Trips an opponent, i.e., throwing or attempting to throw him by the use of the legs or by stooping in front of or behind him;

(c) Jumps at an opponent;

(d) Charges an opponent in a violent or dangerous manner;

(e) Charges an opponent from behind unless the latter be obstructing;

(f) Strikes or attempts to strike an opponent;

(g) Holds an opponent with his hand or any part of his arm;

(h) Pushes an opponent with his hand or any part of his arm;

(i) Handles the ball, i.e., carries, strikes or propels the ball with his hand or arm. (This does not apply to the goalkeeper within his own penalty-area);

shall be penalised by the award of a **direct free-kick-** to be taken by the opposing side from the place where the offence occurred.

Should a player of the defending side intentionally commit one of the above nine offences within the penalty-area he shall be penalised by a **penalty-kick**.

A penalty-kick can be awarded irrespective of the position of the ball, if in play, at the time an offence within the penalty-area is committed.

A player committing any of the five following offences:

1. Playing in a manner considered by the Referee to be dangerous, e.g., attempting to kick the ball while held by the goalkeeper;

2. Charging fairly, i.e., with the shoulder, when the ball is not within playing distance of the players concerned and they are definitely not trying to play it;

3. When not playing the ball, intentionally obstructing an opponent, i.e., running between the opponent and the ball, or interposing the body so as to form an obstacle to an opponent;

4. Charging the goalkeeper except when he
   (a) is holding the ball;
   (b) is obstructing an opponent;
   (c) has passed outside his goal-area;
5. When playing as goalkeeper,
   (a) takes more than 4 steps whilst holding, bouncing or throwing the ball in the air and catching it again without releasing it so that it is played by another player, or
   (b) indulges in tactics which, in the opinion of the Referee, are designed merely to hold up the game and thus waste time and so give an unfair advantage to his own team,

shall be penalised by the award of an- **indirect free-kick-** to be taken by the opposing side from the place where the infringement occurred.

A player shall be- **cautioned-** if:

(j) he enters the field of play to join or rejoin his team after the game has commenced without first having received a signal from the Referee showing him that he is in order to do so.
   If the game has been stopped (to administer the caution) it shall be restarted by the Referee dropping the ball at the place where the infringement occurred, but if the player has committed a more serious offence he shall be penalised according to that section of the Law infringed;

(k) he persistently infringes the Laws of the Game;

(l) he shows by word or action, dissent from any decision given by the Referee;

(m) he is guilty of ungentlemanly conduct.For any of these last three offences, in addition to the caution, an **indirect free-kick** shall also be awarded to the opposing side from the place where the offence occurred. A player shall be -**sent off**- the field of play, if:

(n) in the opinion of the Referee he is guilty of violent conduct or serious foul play;

(o) he uses foul or abusive language;

(p) he persists in misconduct after having received a caution.

If play be stopped by reason of a player being ordered from the field for an offence without a separate breach of the Law having been committed, the game shall be resumed by an **indirect free-kick** awarded to the opposing side from the place where the infringement occurred.

LAW XIII.—FREE-KICK

Free-kicks shall be classified under two heads: "Direct" (from which a goal can be scored direct against the **offending side**), and "Indirect" (from which a goal cannot be scored unless the ball has been played or touched by a player other than the kicker before passing through the goal).

When a player is taking a direct or an indirect free-kick inside his own penalty-area, all of the opposing players shall remain outside the area, and shall be at least ten yards from the ball whilst the kick is being taken. The ball shall be in play immediately it has travelled the distance of its own circumference and is beyond the penalty-area. The goalkeeper shall not receive the ball into his hands, in order that he may thereafter kick it into play. If the ball is not kicked direct into play, beyond the penalty-area, the kick shall be re-taken.

When a player is taking a direct or an indirect free-kick outside his own penalty-area, all of the opposing players shall be at least ten yards from the ball, until it is in play, unless they are standing on their own goal-line, between the goal-posts. The ball shall be in play when it has travelled the distance of its own circumference.

If a player of the opposing side encroaches into the penalty-area, or within ten yards of the ball, as the case may be, before a free-kick is taken, the Referee shall delay the taking of the kick, until the Law is complied with.

The ball must be stationary when a free-kick is taken, and the kicker shall not play the ball a second time, until it has been touched or played by another player.

Punishment. If the kicker after taking the free-kick, plays the ball a second time before it has been touched or played by another player an indirect free-kick shall be taken by a player of the opposing team from the spot where the infringement occurred.

LAW XIV.—PENALTY-KICK

A penalty-kick shall be taken from the penalty-mark and, when it is being taken, all players with the exception of the player taking the kick, and the opposing goalkeeper, shall be within the field of play but outside the penalty-area, and at least 10 yards from the penalty-mark. The opposing goalkeeper must stand (without moving his feet) on his own goal-line, between the goal-posts, until the ball is kicked. The player taking the kick must kick the ball forward; he shall not play the ball a second time until it has been touched or played by another player. The ball shall be deemed in play directly it is kicked, i.e., travelled the distance of its circumference, and a goal may be scored direct from such a penalty-kick. If the ball touches the goalkeeper before passing between the posts, when a penalty-kick is being taken at or after the expiration of half-time or full-time, it does not nullify a goal. If necessary, time of play shall be extended at half-time or full-time to allow a penalty-kick to be taken.

Punishment:

For any infringement of this Law:

(a) by the defending team, the kick shall be retaken if a goal has not resulted

(b) by the attacking team other than by the player taking the kick, if a goal is scored it shall be disallowed and the kick retaken.

(c) by the player taking the penalty-kick, committed after the ball is in play, a player of the opposing team shall take an indirect free-kick from the spot where the infringement occurred.

LAW XV.—THROW-IN

When the whole of the ball passes over a touch-line, either on the ground or in the air, it shall be thrown in from the point where it crossed the line, in any direction, by a player of the team opposite to that of the player who last touched it. The thrower at the moment of delivering the ball must face the field of play and part of each foot shall be either on the touch-line or on the ground outside the touch-line. The thrower shall use both hands and shall deliver the ball from behind and over his head. The ball shall be in play immediately it enters the field of play, but the thrower shall not again play the ball until it has been touched or played by another player. A goal shall not be scored direct from a throw-in.

Punishment: *(a)* If the ball is improperly thrown in the throw-in shall be taken by a player of the opposing team.

(b) If the thrower plays the ball a second time before it has been touched or played by another player, an indirect free-kick shall be taken by a player of the opposing team from the place where the infringement occurred.

LAW XVI.—GOAL-KICK

When the whole of the ball passes over the goal-line excluding that portion between the goal-posts, either in the air or on the ground, having last been played by one of the attacking team, it shall be kicked direct into play beyond the penalty-area from a point within that half of the goal-area nearest to where it crossed the line, by a player of the defending team. A goalkeeper shall not receive the ball into his hands from a goal-kick in order that he may thereafter kick it into play. If the ball is not kicked beyond the penalty-area, i.e., direct into play, the kick shall be retaken. The kicker shall not play the ball a second time until it has touched or been played by another player. A goal shall not be scored direct from such a kick. Players of the team opposing that of the player taking the goal-kick shall remain outside the penalty-area whilst the kick is being taken.

Punishment: If a player taking a goal-kick plays the ball a second time after it has passed beyond the penalty-area, but before it has touched or been played by another player, an indirect free-kick shall be awarded to the opposing team, to be taken from the place where the infringement occurred.

LAW XVII.—CORNER-KICK

When the whole of the ball passes over the goal-line, excluding that portion between the goal-posts, either in the air or on the ground, having last been played by one of the defending team, a member of the attacking team shall kick the ball from within the quarter circle at the nearest corner flag-post, which must not be moved, i.e., a corner-kick. A goal may be scored direct from such a kick. Players of the team opposing that of the player taking the corner-kick shall not approach within 10 yards of the ball until it is in play, i.e., it has travelled the distance of its own circumference, nor shall the kicker play the ball a second time until it has been touched or played by another player.

Punishment: For an infringement of this Law an indirect free-kick shall be awarded to the opposing team, to be taken from the place where the infringement occurred.

Index

AC Milan team, 3
agility exercises, 174
all-star team competition, 188–189
amateur soccer, 153
American soccer. *See* United States,
    soccer in
apprentice professional contract, 195
Archibald, Warren, 162
artificial turf, 167–168
athletic supports, 17
attack, depth in, 127–129, 130
    dribbling on, 127
    penalty area, 127
    three-man formation, 128–129
    width on, 136
    w-m formation, 108
attackers, 18, 23–25, 27
    corner kicks, uses of, 147
    free kicks, uses of, 148–149
    goal area and, 157–158
    position changes of, 122–126
    techniques of, 116–117, 121–151
audience size, 1, 186
Aztec Stadium, 1

back-heading, 65–67
backheel kick, 41–42
back pass, 130
backs. *See* defenders
Bahr, Casey, 189
    Walter, 189
ball, 8–9
ball control, 51–76
    airborne, 53–59
    dribbling, 70–76, 115, 117 180–181,

ball control (cont'd)
    182–183
    drills, 176–177, 180–181
    ground, 52–53
    heading, 60–68
    principles of, 52
    running and, 68–70
    trapping, 51, 53–59
ball possession, 159
    interception, 76–78
    offensive play, 121–151
    shoulder charge, 78, 80
    tackling, 79–85
    tactics, 117–118
Baltimore Bays, 5
banana kick, 39–40, 148
banana shot, 97
Banfield, 3
Barto, Barry, 196
Best, George, 6–7
    John, 85
Blackmore, Richard, 19, 87, 196
body exercises, 174–176
Bradley, Gordon, 5, 30, 162, 195

Cannon, Otey, 196
catching, by goalie, 88–91
chest trap, 57
chipped kick, 37–39, 117, 168
circuit training, 169–176
clearing the ball, 29–30
    goalie's role in, 94–96
    team drills, 184
Cleveland Stokers, 5
college soccer, 3, 187, 191–192, 195,

college soccer (cont'd)
   196
commands, goalie, 104
Concacaf, 188, 189
contact lenses, 17
continuous motion, uses of, 127
controlled passes, 130–132
Copa Libertadores, 189
corner kicks, 14
   attack, uses in, 147
   goalie's role in, 101
Cosmos Soccer Academy, 195
coverage, double, 162
   man-for-man, 107, 181
   shadow, 162
   tight, 162
crossfield switch play, 135–136
Cummings, Everald, 122

Dallas Tornados, 5, 85, 162
Da Rui (player), 87
defenders, 18, 19–23, 27, 117
   techniques of, 114
defense, against dribbling, 73–74
   against free kicks, 161–162
   goal area, 160
   goalie's role in, 160, 162–164
   man-for-man, 153–158
   zone, 107, 153, 154, 166
defensive play, 153–168
   field conditions and, 166–168
   organization, 154–156
   tactics, 156–166
deflection, goalie's skills in, 92–93
   heading, 67
   kick, 42
Dentscher Fussball-Bund, 3
depth in attack, 127–129, 130
diagonal, pass, 130
   runs, 137–138
direct free kick, 11, 148–149
diving header, 65
   saves, 91
double coverage, 162
down the line, 118
downward heading, 65
dribbling, 70–76, 79, 115, 117
   attack, 127
   change of pace, 73
   defense against, 73–74
   individual exercises, 180
   screening, 73, 132–134

dribbling (cont'd)
   showing the ball, 73
   team drills, 181, 182–183
dribbling game, 182–183
drills, ball possession, 181–182
   dribbling, 181, 182–183
   passing, 181, 182
   pre-game, 183–185
   See also exercises; skill practices
drop-ball, 142–144
duration of game, 9
Duvalier, "Papa Doc," 189

engine room personnel, 23, 108
equipment, 8–9, 15–17
European Cup, 189
European teams, 113
Eusebio (player), 97
exercises, agility, 174
   body, 174–176
   circuit training, 169–176
   jumping, 174
   running, 169–174
   See also drills; skill practices

faking, 79, 127. See also dribbling
Federación Mexicana de Fútbol
      Asociación, 3
Fédération Internationale de Football
      Association (FIFA), 3, 4, 110, 111
   duties of, 187–188
field conditions, 166–168
field of play, 8
fielding the ball, 88–91
formations. See systems of play
forward heading, 63–65
Forwards. See attackers
fouling, 11, 78, 85, 149, 165–166
foul throw, 76
4-4-2 system, 111
4-3-3 system, 109–110, 116
4-2-4 system, 106, 108–109, 110, 113,
      116, 121
free kicks, 11–14, 85
   defense against, 161–162
   goalie and, 101–102
   offensive play tactics, 148–149
front block tackle, 80–81
full backs. See defenders

Gaetjens, Joe, 189
glasses, 17

goal area, defense of, 160
goal hanging, 164
goalie, 9, 18, 19, 26, 40
   catching of, 88–91
   clearing, 94–96
   commands, 104
   defensive role of, 160, 162–164
   deflecting skills, 92–93
   drills, 181, 183
   free kicks, role in, 101–102
   penalty kick, role in, 149
   proper positioning, 96–101
   punching, 93
   rules for, 102–103
   smothering, 93–94
   throwing out, 94–96
goal kick, 14

halfbacks. See linkmen
half-field press, 158
half-volley kick, 46
heading, 114, 117
   back-, 65–67
   deflective, 67
   diving header, 65
   downward, 65
   drills, 179–180
   forward, 63–65
   techniques, 60–63
high school soccer, 187
history of soccer, 2–3, 106, 108
Hofstra Stadium, 195
Horton, Randy, 7, 19, 60, 96, 121

indirect free kick, 11, 148–149
in play ball, 9
inside-of-the-foot-kick, 36–37
   trap, 54–55, 59
instep kicks, 30, 31, 32–40
   banana, 39–40, 148
   chipped, 37–39, 137, 168
   inside-of-the-foot, 36–37
   lofted, 32, 35–36
   low drive, 32–35
   swerve-ball, 39–40
in-swinger, 147
interception, 76–78; See also tackling
International Football Association,
   187–188
international offside rule, 108
international soccer, 1–3, 187–189
interval running, 171

jab kick, 42–43
Jairzinho (player), 58
javelin-type throw, 95–96
Jelinek, Josef, 29, 121, 149
Joe Gaetjens Foundation, 189
Jules Rimet Trophy, 188. See also
   World Cup
jumping, exercises, 174
   power, 175

Kerr, John, 19, 116, 149
kick, 29–49
   banana, 39–40, 148
   chipped, 37–39, 117, 168
   corner, 14, 101, 147
   deflection, 42
   diagonal, 130
   free, 11–14, 85, 101–102, 148–149,
     161–162
   goal, 14
   goalie and, 94–96
   half-volley, 46
   inside-of-the-foot, 36–37
   instep, variations, 30, 31, 32–40
   jab, 42–43
   lofted, 32, 35–36
   long volley, 43–44
   low drive, 32–35
   outside-of-the-foot, 40–41
   overhead volley, 46–49
   penalty, 14, 85, 127, 149
   scissors, 46–49
   short volley, 44–46
   swerve-ball, 39–40
   See also pass
kicking-off, 140–142
Kofie, Emanuel, 87

laws of the game, 187
line, blue, 111
   penalty, 110
linkmen, 18, 23, 46
   techniques of, 115–116
lofted kick, 32, 35–36
long pass, 134–135
long volley kick, 43–44
low drive kick, 32–35

Maccabi-Tel-Aviv, 5, 19
Mahy, Barry, 114
man-for-man coverage, defined, 107
   drill, 181

man-for-man defense, 153–158
Maracana Stadium, 1
Mfum, Willie, 122
Miami Toros, 162
midfield play, 117
midfield players. *See* linkmen; systems
of play
Moscow Dynamo, 2–3, 5, 116

National Collegiate Athletic Association
(NCAA), 187, 195
rules, 196
National Professional Soccer League, 4
New York Cosmos, 5, 7, 18, 25–26, 29,
44, 60, 72, 85, 153
defensive play, 166, 167, 169
offensive play, 121–122, 127,
135–136, 142
pre-game drills, 183–185
throw-in maneuver, 145
New York Generals, 5
North American Soccer League
(NASL), 4–5, 7, 16, 87, 110, 111,
121, 128, 147, 162, 166, 169, 193,
196
number of players, 9
numerical advantage, 119–120, 165–166

Oakland Clippers, 5
offensive play, 121–151
building an attack, 126–136
penetration, 136–140
set plays, 140–151
offside, 9–11
blue line, 111
rule, 108, 110, 164–165
trap, 149–151, 165
Olympic Games, 189
1–4–1–4 system, 112–113
one-on-one drill, 181
open space, use of, 139–140
out-of-play ball, 9
outside forwards, 23–25
outside-of-the-foot kicks, 40–41
trap, 55
out-swinger, 147
overhead volley kick, 46–49
overlap runs, 138–139

pacing the game, 134–135
pass, accuracy, 120
back, 130

pass (cont'd)
control, 130–132
diagonal, 130
drills, 178, 181, 182, 184
long, 134–135
reverse, 130
wall, 132–134, 181
See also kick
Pele, 5, 6, 51, 58, 97, 162
biography of, 195–196
penalty area, attack maneuvers, 127
defense of, 160
penalty kick, 14, 85, 127, 149
penalty line, 110
penetration, 136–140
Pennsylvania, University of, 196
personal fitness training, 169–181
Philadelphia Textile Institute, 196
physical fitness. *See* drills; exercises
physique of player, 6–7
players, number of, 9
size of, 6–7
substitute, 9
playing a man short, 165–166
position changes, 122–126
possession. *See* ball possession
power jumping, 175
pre-game drills, 183–185
protective equipment, 16–17
punching, 93

quick retreating defense, 160

referees, 9, 142–144, 165, 166
Renshaw, Mike, 162
retreating defense, quick, 160
slow, 158–160
reverse pass, 130
Rochester (team), 85
Roth, Werner, 22, 85, 114, 166
rules, game, 8–14, 187–188
goalie, 102–103
NCAA, 196
offside, 108, 110, 164–165
running, ball control and, 68–70
diagonal, 137–138
exercises, 169–174
interval, 171
overlap, 138–139

St. Louis Stars, 23, 85, 149, 196
San Francisco University, 196

Santos of Brazil, 5, 162, 195
    See also Pele
scissors kick, 46–49
scoring, 9
Scottish Football Association, 3
screening, 73, 132–134
Seattle, Wash., youth teams in, 194
set plays, 140–151
    corner kick, 101, 147–148
    drop-ball, 142–144
    free kicks, 11–14, 85, 101–102,
        148–149, 161–162
    kick-off, 140–142
    offside trap, 149–151
    penalty kicks, 14, 85, 127, 149
    throw-in, 14, 75–76, 144–147
Sewell, John, 85
shadow coverage, 162
shin guards, 17
shoes, 16
shooting, 97, 129
    individual exercises, 178–179
    team drills, 184
Short, Peter, 85
short volley kick, 44–46
shoulder charge, 78, 80
showing the ball, 73
shuttle passes, 130
side block tackle, 81–82
side-of-the-foot stop, 54
Siega, Jorge, 29, 72, 122
skill practice, ball control, 176–177,
        180–181
    dribbling, 180
    goaltending, 181
    heading, 179–180
    passing, 178
    shooting, 178–179
    See also exercises; drills
sliding tackle, 82–85, 167–168
slow retreating defense, 158–160
smothering, 93–94
soccer, amateur, 153
    college, 3, 187, 191–192, 195–196
    high school, 187
    history of, 2–3, 106, 108
    international, 1–3, 187–189
soccer-style kick. *See* instep kicks
sole-of-the-foot stop, 52–53, 73
sole trap, 55–57
space defense, 153
start of play, 9

Startzel, Stan, 196
strategy, 117–120
strikers. *See* attackers
Stritzl, Siggy, 7, 97, 116, 148
substitutes, 9
sweeper, 112–113
swerved-ball kick, 39–40
switch play, 135–136
system of play, defined, 106
    formations explained, 108–113
    individual player skills, 113–117
    team tactics, 117–120

tackles, 79–85
    front block, 80–81
    side block, 81–82
    sliding, 82–85
team, player skills, 113–117
    practice, 181–185
    tactics, 117–120
thigh trap, 57–58
three-against-one drill, 181
three-man attacking formation,
        128–129
3–2–5 system, 106, 108
throw in, 14, 75–76, 144–147
throwing out, goalie and, 94–96
tight coverage, 162
Tostao (player), 58
Toye, Clive, 5
trap, 51, 53–59
    chest, 57
    exercises, 180–181
    inside-of-the-foot, 54–55, 59
    offside, 149–151, 165
    outside-of-the-foot, 55
    sole, 55–57
    thigh, 57–58
two-against-one drill, 181
two-against-two drill, 181–182
2–3–5 system, 106–107

uneven teams, drill, 182
uniforms, 16–17
United States Soccer Football
    Association (USSFA), 4, 107, 189,
    193
United States, soccer in, 3–5, 189–196

volley control, 181
volley kicking, 43–49
    half-volley, 46

volley kicking (cont'd)
  long volley, 43–44
  overhead volley, 46–49
  short volley, 44–46

wall pass, 132–134, 181
warm-up practice, 183–185
Washington Darts, 97
width on the attack, 136
wind conditions, 168
Winter, Mike, 149

w-m formation, 108
World Cup competition, 58, 188–189, 190

Yashin, Lev, 16, 87
Young, Roby, 19, 122
youth teams, 193–196

Zajdel, Dieter, 116
zone defense, 107, 153, 154, 166